The Fugitive Philosopher

TIMOTHY LEARY

Preface by Fraser Clark
Compiled by Beverly A. Potter

Ronin Publishing
Berkeley Ca

I came to regard Timothy as a true
pioneer of human evolution. He
consolidated ancient psychic wisdoms
and cast them in modern-day terms so
that they could be of use to the spiritual
explorers of the twenty-first century.
—William S. Burroughs

RONIN BOOKS BY TIMOTHY LEARY

High Priest

Chaos & Cyber Culture

The Politics of Ecstasy

Psychedelic Prayers

Change Your Brain

The Politics of Self-Determination

Start Your Own Religion

Your Brain Is God

Turn On Tune In Drop Out

Musings on Human Metamorphoses

Evolutionary Agents

The Politics of PsychoPharmacology

The counter culture Shaman
of the hippie generation.
—*Newsweek*

Dr. Leary is a hero of
American consciousness.
—Allen Ginsberg

The Fugitive Philosopher

Timothy Leary

The Fugitive Philosopher

Published by
Ronin Publishing, Inc.
PO Box 22900
Oakland, CA 94609
www.roninpub.com

Production:

Editor:	Beverly A. Potter, Ph.D. docpotter.com
Cover Design:	Beverly A. Potter
Cover Photo:	From *Intelligence Agents*
Book Design:	Beverly A. Potter

Fonts:

Alien League—Iconian Fonts; Americana—Adobe Sys; Arial—Monotype Corp; Avant Guarde—Apple; Baskerville Old Face—Miscrosoft; Dictator—Chank; FoxScript—J P Be Hart; Golgotha—Chank; Goliath—Fonthead; Malapropism—pizzadude; Marker Felt—Pat Snyder; Navel—Fonthead; Palatino—Apple; Ruthless—Astigmatic; Spirit Medium—Nate Piekos; UncleStinky—Chank; Westsac—Chank; WingDings—Microsoft.

Library of Congress Card Number: 2003098086
Distributed to the book trade by PGW/Perseus
Printed in the United States by Inner Workings

The Fugitive Philosopher was derived from *Intelligence Agents* intersperced with brief excerpts, by permission of Ronin Publishing, from *High Priest, The Politics of Ecstasy, Turn On Tune In Drop Out, Psychedelic Prayers, Musings on Human Metamorphoses; Change Your Brain, Start Your Own Religion, Your Brain Is God, The Politics of PsychoPharmacology; The Politics of Self-Determination; Chaos & Cyber Culture, Changing My Mind Among Others,* and brief fair use quotes and paraphrases from *Flashbacks*.

TABLE OF CHAPTERS

LEARY PHILOSOPHIES

Preface

TiMOTHY LEARY WAS A SAiNT

by Fraser Clark

*L*eary was a professor of psychology when he discovered psilocybin, and later LSD. He quickly realized that psychedelics were a powerful tool for improving mental health and spiritual development. He was vocal in this belief. He was fired by Harvard University for his experiments. He was harassed and demonized. He was arrested and imprisoned. He escaped with the help of a rebel underground and fled to Europe and Africa. Through all of this he refused to shut up about the importance of psychedelics as the Primary Tool to Save the World.

Saying Timothy Leary was a Saint is not as strong as it appears. Saint Nicolas—Santa Claus—was a saint because he was a lovely, jolly man who gave presents to children. That's kind of what Tim was for us hippies. He was a Saint Claus who brought hope and inspiration to so many people.

One definition of Saint is "pre-eminent for holiness". If holiness includes shrugging off well-paid middle class security **Tim Leary will be remembered long after Jesus, Mohammed and Elvis are forgotten.** to suffer the tribulations of working for humanity in a world controlled by the dark forces of Ego, Power and Dominance, then Saint Timothy was certainly "pre-eminent for holiness".

Predecessor of Rave Scene

Another definition of saint is "an illustrious predecessor." Timothy Leary is unquestionably a direct predecessor of today's global shamanic rave scene. Yes, it would have happened eventually, but it might have taken another hundred years if it were not for both LSD and for Tim Leary refusing to shut up about it. And the world needs the healing insights of psychedelics *more than ever* today.

Rave isn't something brand new that came out of nowhere. The Hippy Spirit of Free Shamanic Inner Enquiry was reborn, in far larger numbers, when rave burst upon the world.

So, in terms of illustrious predecessors, Ken Kesey, Ginsberg, the Beatles, and Elvis were Heroes. Timothy Leary, however, rises a level above to that of Sainthood.

Timothy Leary was a human being of his time. He had as many failings and repressed material as any of his contemporaries. *Of course*, he made mistakes; *maybe* he sinned, *maybe* even seriously. But with today's communications technology we know more about six months in Leary's life than in the whole lifetime of Santa Claus. We shall never know if Santa Claus was a secret pedophile, but we know a million details about Leary—many of which are untrue. Let's not miss the Big Picture of the man's life by losing ourselves in a mass of shabby alleged details. How would you fare if the glare of the world's media were set loose on you—especially if the mass of that media is serving Mammon?

Let's not miss the Big Picture of the man's life.

—**Fraser Clark**
Parallel-Youniversity
www.parallel-youniversity.com/fraser

Introduction

THERE ARE
24 TIMOTHY LEARYS

i'm sure that you have read many lurid accounts of my activities. As a well-trained Out-Caste, I plead *nolo contendere.* That's a satirical reference to the case of CIA Director Richard Helms who pleaded *nolo contendere* to indictments for lying to Congress. Can you imagine that? Actually lying to Congress?!

I want you to know that I encourage all rumors hostile or adulatory—as badges of honor. I'm going to confide something on a need-to-know basis about facts that clarify the images and media hypes that have been circulating around my name that I'm not sure the general public is ready for.

> I encourage all rumors hostile or adulatory—as badges of honor.

Since our Harvard experiments, there have been 24 Timothy Learys running around the world, playing parts in the 24 Reality Movies of the period. Remember this: it's your nervous system that creates and controls your reality. You dial and tune the images you wish. So pick out the Timothy Leary image you want. There's probably no insanity, eccentricity, immorality, heroic divinity or messianic omnipotence that hasn't been attributed to one of these images. But that's the standard fate of Out-Castes.

In his biography of my life, *I Have America Surrounded*, John Higgs revealed keen insight when he noted that I avoided imposing myself—my personality, my games—on people. Instead, when meeting new people I let **Do not** them project their interpretations of me onto me. **believe** In this way I could be all things to all people. I **anything** may be a friend, a scientist, a charlatan—a lot **I say.** of folks went for that reality tunnel—a genius, a cad, or an irresponsible idiot.

I must clarify something. *Please do not believe anything I say.* By all means listen to everything; consider anything. Pick up a belief and try it out. If it works, use it as long as it work. And then put it down or change it. Be open to new ideas. But I urge you, don't believe in any final sense anything I say.

I studied human nervous systems for just about my entire professional life. I performed many neurological experiments and came to the conclusion that the human nervous system—this 111-billion-cell-bio-electric computer—is not a set of ice tongs. You don't hook sharp claws of belief onto an idea and hold it.

Intelligence Agents

In 1960, Out-Caste agents started circulating the rumor that Intelligence was the most important factor in human life. They said: "What else do you value? Love? Virtue? Money? Power? Freedom? Truth? All of these can be enhanced by increasing intelligence. **You dial and tune** A failure to increase intelligence can **the images you wish.** only diminish our ability to obtain and enjoy these goods."

In this book I'm going to talk to you as one intelligent person to another about evolution of intelligence. My purpose is to recruit you as Intelligence Agents—Change Agents, Out-Castes.

There are many social and genetic forces designed to resist change and retard intelligence increase. I certainly am not complaining. When I talk about the forces that discourage change, I emphasize that Repressive Hive-Bureaucracy is a genetic and social necessity. The good-old-bulls who run the herd are robot-programmed to scare you about change. Their salaried hive-function is to tell you, "Stay close to the center of the herd. Don't get too far out or you'll be an Out-Caste—oh my gawd! Don't get too far in front or you'll get picked off. Stick close to the home base. Don't rock the gene-ship. Avoid change."

Out-Castes are cast out, thrown forward, pushed up, above and beyond, contemporary hive realities.

That's okay. Neither a species nor a social-gene-pool can lurch off in one direction after another, aimlessly, as each mutation comes along. There has to be some preservative central tendency. I honor and respect the conservative forces in society and the DNA code that puts brakes on change. At the same time it is my genetic duty to spray you with Electronically Amplified Brain Waves designed to activate you, to cut you loose for all-out, post-hive change.

Out-Castes

Certain human beings are pre-selected, usually without their awareness, from each gene-pool, to have neural circuits activated that fabricate future realities. Future gene-pools. These individuals are

I'm not Timothy Leary. I just use his identity.
–Testimony to Senate Hearing
The Politics of PsychoPharmacology

Out-Castes surf the ripples of history. genetically templated to live much of the time in the future. They are, to this extent, alienated from current hive realities.

Because most of these agents are unaware of their genetic assignment they feel agonizingly out of step. Some are shunned and even locked up by the gene-pools they serve. Those who are lucky enough to recognize their post-human genetic caste attain a level of great prescience and humorous insight. They understand that they are Time Travelers, literally walking around in past civilizations. A most entertaining and effective role to play. While they have little power to change the ripples of history or the waves of evolution—they can surf them with increasing skill.

Such Evolutionary Agents are best described as Out-Castes. They are cast out, thrown forward, pushed up, above and beyond, contemporary hive realities.

As evolution accelerates there are more and more Evolutionary Agents emerging. In the 1960s it was probably true that every gene-pool cast out its futique agents. We are now learning to identify these Out-Castes and benefit from their contribution to the species.

–Intelligence Agents

1
FROM
THE BEGINNING

i was born in Springfield, Massachusetts—an
only child. My father was an Irish American dentist
who took off when I was 13. I attended three different colleges, including two years at the College of the Holy
Cross in Worcester, Massachusetts where I was constantly
in trouble for cutting classes, drinking and chasing girls. I
was a normal, red-blooded, horny guy. The
scholastic approach to religion didn't turn
me on. At the age of nineteen, I distressed
my Roman Catholic mother by abandoning
Holy Cross two years before graduation.
Few would have predicted that I would
emerge as a religious leader, let alone as a rebel with a cause.

> **The scholastic approach to religion didn't turn me on.**

After much badgering by my mother, I transferred to
West Point. It was a bad move. You could say that my interests were philosophic rather than militaristic. I was kicked
out after 18 months. Actually, I was forced to resign because
I was caught lying about smuggling liquor into a sports
event. Not until I transferred to the University of Alabama
did I begin to settle down academically to earn a B.A. in psychology. It was THE WAR so I enlisted in the Army. I got a
master's degree from Washington State University in 1946.

After my discharge from the service in 1946, I accepted a well-paying fellowship to graduate school at the University of California in Berkeley where I earned my doctorate in psychology in 1950. The funding came from the Veterans Administration, an obvious spin-off of the War Department.

Big Brother, Big Money

During the first week of training, the graduate fellows were assembled to meet a representative from Washington who announced, with considerable solemn satisfaction, that the Federal Government was getting into psychology in a big way. Enormous grants of money for salaries and research could be expected.

This prediction was no exaggeration. Before World War II, psychological research was a gentleman's game of little interest to Big Brother and thus with almost no bureaucratic funding or supervision. After the War, federal support of psychologists in the form of fellowships, salaried posts and research grants became the dominating fact of university life.

What Did Money Buy?

The federal bureaucracy paid for and bought American psychology. What did this money buy? Exactly what Big Brother wanted—a science of adjustment and control. Branches of psychology that study management of human behavior—clinical psychology, personality psychology, social psychology—leaped into prominence:.

Leadership and direction of these new fields was assumed by former CIA functionaries, wise in the ways of government support. The field of personality psychology in particular was covered with CIA fingerprints.

Professor Harry Murray, wartime director of the CIA Psychological Project, assembled at his Harvard center the cream of personality researchers. The aim was to investigate, not clinical pathologies because teams of government-supported psychiatrists were already gleefully taking

What kind of society will we have if we deprive young people of the right to aimless exploration, wandering, curious poking around, unskilled experiments in new forms of communication?
–The Politics of PsychoPharmacology

care of that. No, the aim was to assess normal and successful humans.

By 1950 most of Murray's staff had fanned out to universities throughout the country in posts of executive power. Donald McKinnon, for example, organized the Institute of Personality Assessment and Research at the University of California in Berkeley (IPAR). To IPAR came Air Force officers and creative, successful subjects from many professions to participate in weekend assessments based directly on CIA methods. IPAR was funded by the Ford Foundation, the U.S. Government, and God knows how many fronts.

IPAR

In spite of the prestige, affluence and power of its staff, IPAR never published any important papers, never had to compete for funding and seemed to be, like some Soviet rower, isolated from the exciting self-revolution in personality that occurred from 1950 to 1976. This is not to say that the IPAR psychologists and administrators were idle. Plenty was going on. IPAR was "running" American psychology—monitoring the field, quietly screening new ideas and promising recruits emerging from the graduate ranks, arranging back-scene support for useful researchers, lining up exchanges of staff with selected foreign depart-

ments. IPAR psychologists kept popping up in the funniest places. One energetic post-doc went along on an Ever-
est climb. Not a bad place to surveil China.

Another profoundly significant IPAR project attempted
to institute Brave New World psych-tech control. A crew-
cut, pink-cheeked church-going staff-member named Har-
rison Gough designed a personality questionnaire to diagnose "normal and superior" persons. The test had scales
for "rebelliousness-conformity" or anti-hive thinking—independence—and so forth.

Gough received a lot of publicity when he floated the
proposal that personality questionnaires could be given to

**American psychol-
ogy was as much a
captive of the CIA as
Russian psychology
was of the KGB.**

every school child in the country
in the first grade. It would then
be possible, claimed Gough, to
pinpoint at age seven, potential
troublemakers and future talented
specialists. Specialized training
and surveillance could then be
instituted from the earliest years. No outcry arose from
the liberal psychologists, which was interesting. Although
the average psychologist was a good-natured, reasonably
progressive person, and although psychologists would be
expected to understand human castes and hive-thought-
control interventions, the profession was, by and large,
amazingly innocent and unconcerned about the fact that it
has been controlled by the federal bureaucracy for decades.

From 1920 to 1960 American psychology was as much a
captive of the CIA as Russian psychology was of the KGB.
In some ways American psychology was more co-opted,
because everyone in and out of the Soviet Union knew
what the KGB was doing, but well-paid American psychologists were blandly unaware of their sponsor-masters.
However, when the American Psychological Revolution exploded in the 1960s all this was changed completely.

—Intelligence Agents

2

HIVE CUSTODIANS

During my first month of graduate training, I placed the University of California psychology faculty under intense surveillance. I read their papers and books, dropped in on lectures, observed their behavior. I reluctantly came to the conclusion that these decent, sincere men with corporate smiles were hive custodians whose function it was to prevent change, discourage intelligence increase, and to protect the gene-pool system that protects them.

I spent almost no time on the campus during my four years of graduate training and, thus aloof, received straight "A" grades and was given the prestigious Phi Beta Kappa award.

Having observed how graduate schools brainwash students, I was not surprised that at the time of graduation virtually everyone in my class of twenty-five doctoral students was interested only in finding jobs with easy tenure, profitable outside consulting, mild climate, and good pension plans. Only I and one other flamboyant Irish preterite and classmate named Frank Barron were interested in changing things. We were passionate about the possibility of raising the intelligence of self and others.

The faculty were hive custodians expected to prevent change and discourage intelligence increase.

Avoiding university faculties like the plague, I started my own research project, and for seven years, received funds from the hive central bureaucracy to support my investigations in group therapy and interpersonal diagnosis. The work was *highly praised.* Each year, a soviet-like official would visit my projects, inspect the data and raise my funding. I was amused one time when a purchase order came from the CIA to obtain copies of tests I had developed.

The funding stopped around the time that I found it therapeutic to teach patients how personality tests were **Patients' diagnoses of doctors were more reliable than therapists' diagnoses of patients.** used. My gawd, did I say "patients"?! I trained patients to diagnose themselves and others—including their therapists. The bureaucracy was decidedly not interested in the finding that patients' diagnoses of their therapists were more reliable than therapists' diagnoses of their patients.

Group Therapy Threat

Then there was the group therapy controversy. At that time psychiatrists—who have M.D.s and thusly hold the highest power—were resisting the attempts of psychologists—who have Ph.D.s and hold less power—to diagnose and treat patients. But when faced with a threat, however, both hive-bureaucracies forgot their differences and closed ranks to oppose group therapy, which they viewed as a dangerous method in which the fragile, delicate, easily-destroyed personalities of patients were being tampered with by *other* patients. Patients, later to be called "clients", were preterite, non-elect persons, non-bureaucrats, non-salary, non-experts.

But wait a minute. There's a contradiction here. If Freudian academicians claimed that personality cannot

be changed, then why was it dangerous
for non-medical or non-expertise people
to participate in the therapeutic-process?
If personality is unchanging, what harm
could be done?

The old Judeo-Christian dogma had the
answer. Personality, they taught, could disinte-
grate and change for the worse, but it could not change
for the better, grow, or develop. Why not? Because the
unconscious is bad. Because, as Freud pointed out, society
and ego are frail paper-clip-rubber-band structures flimsily
holding off the basic wickedness of humanity—original
sin. The dutiful stoic mythos of System-People, the managers, who shoulder the burden of gene-pool maintenance,
is always the same. Keep the lid on. Discourage change.
Encourage social adjustment and hive conformity.

—Intelligence Agents

Do **caterpillars** know they will become butterflies?

*—Musings on Human
Metamorphoses*

Embrace Change

*U*nderstand "roots". Intelligence Agents (Out-Castes) study history very carefully. Because we can't navigate precisely into the future unless we understand the rhythms and coherence of past voyages. However, once we've traced our roots back, **Become** it's necessary to move on to the future and **comfort-** create blossoms. Philosophers demonstrate **able with** understanding of the past by the accuracy of **the idea of** their predictions about the future. The time **change.** has come to take a look into the future and catch the next waves that are coming. Watch out! They're going to be big ones.

Three DNA Change Techniques

1) Mutation—a species getting smarter;

2) Metamorphosis—individuals getting more intelligent;

3) Migration—because every time you improve, every time you change, every time some new challenge increases your intelligence, you have to migrate to find new space to live out your new capacity, to custom-make your new vision. Mobility is the classic stimulus for Intelligence Increase, I^2.

Become comfortable with the idea of change. To discover who we are means that we must learn how our intelligence has evolved.   *–Intelligence Agents*

DO NOT LET THEM SCARE YOU ABOUT CHANGE.

Irish Mutants

The **British Empire** performed extraordinary feats of genetic transportation in the 19th century—squirting sperm-egg cargoes around the globe. By moving their Protestant Dom-Species from Scotland, they ruthlessly compressed the Catholic-feudal culture of the Emerald Isle. Faced with loss of the land, Catholic gene-pools were forced to migrate. Each Irish family selected its most intelligent, mobile, adaptable, attractive member to send "across the water". Thus occurred one of the most successful genetic experiments in planetary history. America was flooded with sperm-egg units carefully selected for mobility-nobility.

The first generation of Irish migrants threw railroads across the continent. The second generation became politicians, policers, power functionaries. The third generation, which blossomed after World War II, produced the first Irish-American generation of philosopher-scientists.

Innovative Irish Savants

The brilliant, innovative Irish savants who emerged in the 1930 to 1970 period replaced Jewish intellectuals. Before 1950 Jewish intellectuals carried the neuro-genetic signal. Since Jews were born Out-Castes they were able to transcend hive limits and fabricate new realities. After World War II Jewish culture became hive-establishment—the role of genetic exploration fell to the Irish. The American Celts were prepared perfectly to play the role of Intelligent Agents because of their intellectual history. In pre-migration Ireland the active intellectual person was forced into rebellion. The only educational choices for

Barron Gem: The creative person is both more primitive and more cultivated, more destructive, a lot madder and a lot saner, than the average person.

Barron Gem: The refusal to choose is a form of choice; disbelief is a form of belief. a smart young Irishman were the alien, Rome-oriented feudal priesthood or the academies of the enemy Protestants. Irish women had no educational avenues open to them. Irish brains were thus encouraged to be anti-hive. From this Out-Caste position they were able to create new post-hive realities.

My grad school classmate, Frank Barron's career illustrates the Irish Renaissance. After arriving in America, his ancestors avoided the priest-run ghettoes of the Atlantic Seaboard by moving to the rough frontier of the Pennsylvania mining mountains.

Frank Barron recognized his mutant status at an early age. When the opportunity presented itself, he carried his seed-supply to the California frontier. After obtaining his degree he quickly became a central figure in American psychology, taking over the position previously held by William James. Barron was always the lonely champion of the individual at a time when psychology was totally dedicated to adjustment-conformity. His publications on creativity, innovation, hallucinogenic drugs, and psycho-biography helped push the primitive field of psychology into scientific status.

Barron Gem: Never take a person's dignity: it is worth everything to them, and nothing to you.

–Intelligence Agents

> Almost all intellectual breakthroughs have been produced by mavericks pushed out of and operating independently of establishment knowledge systems.
>
> –Thomas Kuhn
> Quoted in *Flashbacks*

3
GAME'S EYE VIEW

My first job after graduate school was as an assistant professor at UC Berkeley, which I held from 1950 until 1955. That's when my first wife, Marianne, committed suicide, leaving me a single father with two kids—a son and daughter. In 1955 I became director of psychiatric research at the Kaiser Family Foundation.

By most standards, I was a success. But I was actually an anonymous institutional employee who drove to work each morning in a long line of commuter cars and drove home each night and drank martinis like several million other middle-class, liberal, intellectual robots. As it became obvious to me that traditional psychiatric methods hurt as many patients as they helped, I resigned from Kaiser in 1958.

I looked successful on the outside but I was actually just a robot.

I became a lecturer in clinical psychology at Harvard where I evolved my theory of social interplay and personal behavior as so many stylized "games"—a theory subsequently popularized by Dr. Eric Berne in his bestselling book, *Games People Play*. I raised eyebrows right away by sending my students to study emotional problems such as alcoholism where they germinate, rather than in the textbook or the laboratory. Predictably enough, few of these novel notions went over very well with my hidebound colleagues at Harvard.

Game Theory

Game Theory was a very subversive, meta-social concept that implies you are not just the role that you—and society—have fabricated for you. It encourages flexibility, humorous detachment from social pressures. It allows you to change "games" and positions without the shame-stigma of being unreliable or undependable. It allows people to measure their performances and to seek coaching. It endorses change-ability and an amused-cynical liberation from hive pressures. Game Theory subtly undermines the cultural authoritarianism that forces people to play rigid parts in games that they themselves do not select.

My colleagues tried to discount my observations as being frivolous. However many sports, or "play-games", are superior in their behavior-change techniques to psychiatry and psychology. Take the game of American baseball. Baseball officials classify and reliably record molecular behavior—bit sequences such as strikes, hits, double plays, and so forth. Their compiled records convert into indices for summarizing and predicting behavior. Runs Batted In (RBI) and Earned-Run Average (ERA) are two obvious examples. To judge events that are not obviously and easily coded, baseball employs well-trained umpires.

Tunnel vision has always narrowed the academic mind.

Baseball experts have devised another remarkable set of techniques for bringing about desired results: coaching. Baseball shares time and space with learners, sets up role models, feeds relevant information back to the learner, for endless practice. Baseball is clean and successful because it is seen as a game. You can shift positions. You know how you are doing. You can quit or declare yourself a free agent.

Cultural stability is maintained by preventing people from seeing that the roles, rules, goals, rituals, language, and values of society are game structures. Cultural institutions encourage the delusion that games have inevitable givens, involving unchangeable laws of behavior. It is treason not to play the nationality game, the racial game, the religious game. A person who can stand outside or above his or her culture—an Out Caste—can often cut through game-rules to what is most relevant to survival and peace of mind.

The Behavior-Change Game

Like baseball and basketball, the behavior that psychiatrists label as "disease" can be considered a game, too. Dr. Thomas Szasz suggested that the psychiatric condition that Freud called "hysteria" is a certain doctor-patient game involving deceitful helplessness. Psychiatry and psychology, according to this model, are behavior-change games.

Peter Gould: Tim Leary 1966, from *Psychedelic Prayers*

The popular method of behavior change called psychotherapy interprets confusion and inefficiency in game-playing as illness. Consider the football player who doesn't know the rules. Perhaps he picks up the ball and runs off the field. Shall we pronounce him sick and call the doctor? Not understanding the game nature of behavior leads to confusion and eventual helplessness.

I proposed that when people come to a psychologist asking for help in changing their behavior, that we should find out what games they are caught up in and what games they want to commit themselves to. Treatment should be to expose them to models of successful game-playing for them to emulate and give them objective appraisals of their performance.

Acid Unplugs the Game

The visionary brain-change, consciousness-altering experience is the key to behavior change. All the learned games of life can be seen as programs that select, censor, and thus dramatically limit the available cortical response. Our potentials are much greater than the social-hive games in which we are so blindly trapped. Once the game structure of behavior is seen, change in behavior can occur with dramatic spontaneity.

With the aid of a powerful enthogen like psilocybin or LSD and a skilled guide, local games that frustrate and torment can be seen in the broader, evolutionary dimension. Consciousness-expanding drugs unplug these narrow programs, the social ego, the game-machinery. And with the ego and mind unplugged, what is left? Not the "id"; no dark, evil impulses. These alleged negative "forces" are simply taboos, anti-rules. What is left is something that Western culture knows little about—the uncensored cortex, activated, alert and open to new realities, new imprints.

Why is this brain-activating experience so strange and horrid to Western culture? Perhaps because our Western world is overcommitted to objective, external behavior games. This is a natural opposition: "the game" versus "the meta-game." Behavior versus consciousness. The universal brain-body versus the local cultural-mind.

Intelligence increase stimulated by brain-change is, to me, one of the great-

Consciousness-expanding drugs unplug these narrow programs, the social ego, the game-machinery.

est challenges of our times. What should provoke intense and cheerful competition too often evokes suspicion, anger, impatience.

But in the absence of relevant scientific rituals to handle the drug experience, physicians seek to impose their game of control and prescription. Bohemians naturally impose their games of back-alley secrecy. Police naturally move in to control and prosecute.

Those who talk about the games of life are invariably seen as frivolous anarchists tearing down the social structure. Actually, only those who see culture as a game can appreciate the exquisitely complex magnificence of what human beings have done.

Those of us who play the game of "applied mysticism" respect and support good gamesmanship. Pick out your game, learn the rules, rituals, concepts; play fairly and cleanly. Anger and anxiety are irrelevant, because you see your small game in the context of the great evolutionary game in which no one can lose.

The most effective approach to behavior change is applied neurologic or self-programmed brain-change. Identify the game structure of the event. Make sure that you do not apply the rules and concepts of other games to this situation. Move directly to solve the problem.   *—Change Your Brain*

> **Pick out your game, learn the rules, rituals, concepts; play fairly and cleanly.**

> There's an ominous tendency to call "insane" those we don't agree with.
>
> *—The Politics of PsychoPharmacology*

Psychology Goes to War

P **revious to 1939** murderous-muscular strength, animal aggressiveness and obedient stupidity were the glorious characteristics of warriors. *Gravity's Rainbow* by Thomas Pynchon described in chilling macabre detail how, during World War II, psychology became a basic weapon of warfare and counter-intelligence.

But, as the sensory and motor aspects of belligerence came to depend on intermediate-technology, i.e., machines operated by human minds, a terrible thing happened: Intelligence and mental-caste became factors in warfare! Special endowments beyond brute stupidity, treacherous cunning and unimaginative persistence became survivally attractive.

The brilliant scientist turned mystic, John Lilly, fled from the establishment when he realized that the military had used his research to create bomb-carrying donkeys and dolphins. Lilly mapped the pain and pleasure centers in the brain. The war makers inserted remote-controlled electrodes into donkey brains and strapped bombs onto their

John Lilly's research was used to create bomb-carrying donkeys.

backs and sent them out to traverse through mountains to deliver their payload. When they wandered from the path, a remote zap to the pain center caused a quick correction; followed by a rewarding zap to the pleasure center. Just simple Skinnerian principles. The disillusionment of this realization is what pushed Lilly over the brink to be a self-elected Out-Caste.

The "geniuses" of World War I were primitive herd-animals—a mutation's quantum distance from the scope, acceleration and relativistic adaptability of our current mediocrity. Black Jack Pershing? Teddy Roosevelt? Kaiser Wilhelm? Sgt. York?

By 1939, the selection of killer-teams involved careful screening for inborn caste differences, genetic types, prudently called personality traits or aptitudes. Military psychology became an integral part of the Anglo-American German war machines. The task: identification, assessment, selection, guidance, training, motivation of caste abilities.

Diagnosis and treatment of psychological casualties—an entirely new concept of human nature—also developed. Machines break down; personalities could not break down until personality types were defined by our new mechanical civilization. All our external technology services are a model to understand internal—somatic-neurological—technology. Machines help us to understand our own bodily mechanics. Electronic computers lead us to understand and control our own brains.

Wars End

The problem with military technology is, of course, that wars end. But terrestrial bureaucracies persevere, particularly those of the winning side. The reason post-WWII losers—Germany and Japan—rebounded more rapidly than did the winners—England, France, and Russia—is that the bureaucracies of the losers were destroyed. Anything that destroys a bureaucracy enhances evolution.

So after World War II, the massive industries that had geared up to produce war tools were converted to civilian goods. The managers and technical boys were ready to convert the assembly lines from tanks to fin-tailed cars. The radar factories were converted to manufacture televisions.

WWII losers recovered faster than winners did because their bureaucracies were destroyed. America in the 1950s went on the biggest materialism spree in history.

The wartime psychological technology was also converted to civilian consumption. Personality assessment techniques were taken over by the managerial powers—used to select and train employees. A new gigantic industry emerged employing clinical psychologists and counselors and a new social-moral concept of human nature: adjustment.

1950s Psychology

The aim of personality/clinical psychology and psychiatry during the 1950s was hive-adjustment and the preservation of the past—the prevention of change. To understand the gravity of the situation, remember: there was no concept of personal change in the 1950s. Human personality was seen as a fixed quality that could and should be adjusted to the system. Old-style psychiatrists—formerly called alienists—guarded the psychotic. The radical wing—psychoanalysis—taught that after five years of intensive treatment, five hours a week patients might get enough insight to wearily adjust and to discuss their neurosis at cocktail parties.

The aim of 1950s psychology was hive-adjustment, preservation of the past—prevention of change.

–Intelligence Agents

Your moment-to-moment interpersonal signals pull, fabricate, create the personal environment you inhabit.

Interpersonal Wheel
–The Politics of Self-Determination

The peril of **LSD** resides in its eerie
power to release ancient, wise, at time,
even holy sources of energy.

—The Politics of PsychoPharmacology

4
MY FIRST TRIP

*L**ife Magazine* **ran an article in 1957** by R.
Gordon Wasson documenting the use of psilocybin
mushrooms by indigenous Mazatec people of Mexico
in their religious ceremonies. Anthony Russo, who had
tried the mushroom during a trip to Mexico, gave me an
amazing account of the experience. I was fascinated. I had
to try the "magic" mushrooms.

On a sunny Saturday afternoon in 1960, beside the
swimming pool of my rented summer villa in Cuernavaca,
I ate a handful of odd-looking mushrooms I'd bought from
a witch doctor in a nearby village. Within minutes, I felt
myself being swept over the edge of a sensory Niagara
into a maelstrom of transcendental visions
and hallucinations. The next five hours
can be described in many extravagant
metaphors, but it was above all and without
question the deepest religious experience of
my life.

The implications of that fateful first communion are as yet unmeasured; that they are
both far-reaching and profound, however, is
generally conceded—for the fungi were the
legendary "sacred mushrooms" that have

since become known, and feared by many, as one of the
psychedelic—literally, mind-manifesting—chemicals that
created a national fad among the young and a scandal in
It was the the press. Since then I have found myself
deepest transmogrified from scientist and researcher
deepest into progenitor and high priest of a revolu-
religious tionary movement spawned, not by an idea
experience but by a substance that's been called "the
of my life. spiritual equivalent of the hydrogen bomb".

    I learned more about my brain and its
possibilities in those few glorious hours and more about
psychology during that first trip than I had learned during
all of the years of my graduate studies. I couldn't wait to
"turn on" Richard Alpert when I got back at Harvard.

Outrage

My colleagues' rumblings of skepticism rose to
a chorus of outrage when I returned to Harvard from my
pioneering voyage into inner space—beside the swimming
pool in Cuernavaca—to begin experimenting on myself,
my associates and hundreds of volunteer subjects with
measured doses of psilocybin, the chemical derivative of
the sacred mushrooms.

    I vowed to dedicate the rest of my life as a psychologist
to the systematic exploration of this new instrument. I and
my rapidly multiplying followers began to turn on with
the other psychedelics—morning glory seeds, nutmeg,
marijuana, peyote, mescaline, and
LSD. A hundred times stronger
than psilocybin, LSD sent hal-
lucinated users on multihued,
multileveled roller-coaster rides
so spectacular that it soon became
my primary tool for research.
And as word circulated about
the fantastic phantasmagorical

"trips" taken by my students, it soon became a clandestine campus kick and by 1962 "dropping acid" had become an underground cult among the young avant-garde from London to Los Angeles.

A Pact

I made a pact with DNA, Higher Intelligence. It was the standard contract. I was to illuminate, raise intelligence, transmit all revelations as directly as possible. I was to cling to no former security or comfort, risk the loss of every attachment, accept total responsibility for the realities that emerged. The unspecific compensation would be intrinsic in the intelligence attained.

There was no consuming emotional reaction, no Mosaic thunderbolt. It was, on the contrary, a quiet moment of telepathic communion. There was certainly no visionary presence, no certainty. As fast as my mind would create a self-congratulatory posture, the lens would zoom in to an embarrassing closeup or zoom out to a comic cosmic perspective.

It was part of my assignment, from time to time, when diplomatically graceful, to ask people: Do you believe in a Higher Intelligence, a Master Plan?

The malaise was philosophic. It's my job to produce a new blueprint. But anyone can volunteer for the job. If philosophic bases for human action were made explicit, confusion, apathy, and conflict would vanish. People now avoid philosophic clarification because they fear

It was my job to produce a new blueprint.

the horror of the existential confrontation, the terror of the responsibility of explaining life. Since the sixties we've been involved in a philosophic renaissance; we must make it fashionable, amusing, safe to focus on the galactic perspective.

–Excerpt from "She Comes in Colors" Playboy, 9/66, *The Politics of Ecstasy*

Turn On, Tune In, Drop Out

You are

a God.

Live like one!

−Your Brain Is God

Psychedelic Prayer

VI-5

The Lesson
of Water

What one values in the game is the play.
What one values in the form is the moment of forming.
What one values in the house is the moment of dwelling.
What one values in the heart is the beating.
What one values in the action is the timing.
Indeed
Because you flow like water
You can neither win nor lose.

—Psychedelic Prayers

The Oracle, December 16, 1966, Regent Press

The Religious EXperience

*T*he religious eXperience is the ecstatic, incontrovertibly certain, subjective discovery of answers to seven basic spiritual questions. There can be, of course, absolute subjective certainty in regard to secular questions: Is this the girl I love? Is Fidel Castro a wicked man? Are the Yankees the best baseball team?

Issues which do not involve the seven basic questions belong to secular games, and such convictions and faiths, however deeply held, can be distinguished from the religious. Liturgical practices, rituals, dogmas, theological speculations, can be, and too often are, secular, i.e., completely divorced from the spiritual experience.

The Seven Basic Spiritual Questions

1. *The Ultimate Power Question*—What is the basic energy underlying the universe—the ultimate power that moves the galaxies and nucleus of the atom? Where and how did it all begin? What is the cosmic plan? Field of study: Cosmology.

2. *The Life Question*—What is life? Where and how did it begin? How is it evolving? Where is it going? Field of study: Genesis, biology, evolution, genetics.

3. *The Human Being Question*—Who are we? Whence did we come? What is our structure and function? Field of study: Anatomy and physiology.

4. *The Awareness Question*—How do we sense, experience, know? Field of study: Epistemology, neurology.

5. *The Ego Question*—Who am I? What is my spiritual, psychology, social place in the plan? What should I do about it? Field of study: Social psychology.

6. *The Emotional Question*—What should I feel about it? Psychiatry. Field of study: Personality psychology.

7. *The Ultimate Escape Question*—How can I get out of it? Field of study: Anesthesiology—amateur or professional. Eschatology

An important fact about these questions is that they are continually being answered and re-answered, by all the religions of the world as well as by the data of the natural sciences. Unhappily science and religion are too often diverted toward secular games-goals. Various pressures demand that laboratory and church forget these basic questions and instead provide distractions, illusory protections, narcotic comfort. Most of us dread confrontation with the answers to these basic questions, whether the answers come from objective science or from subjective religion. But if "pure" science and religion address themselves to the same basic questions, what is the distinction between the two disciplines?

Science is the systematic attempt to record and measure the energy process and the sequence of energy transformations we call life. The goal is to answer basic questions in terms of objective, observed, public data. Religion is the systematic attempt to provide answers to the same questions subjectively, in terms of direct, incontrovertible, personal experience.

Psychedelic Prayers

Science is a social system which evolves roles, rules, rituals, values, language, space-time locations to further the quest for these goals, to answer these questions objectively, externally. Religion is a social system which has evolved in roles, rules, rituals, values, language, space-time locations to further the pursuit of the same goals, to answer these questions subjectively through the revelatory experience.

A science which fails to address itself to these spiritual goals, which accepts other purposes—however popular, becomes secular, political and tends to oppose new data. A religion which fails to provide direct experiential answers to these spiritual questions—which fails to produce ecstatic high—becomes secular, political and tend to oppose individual revelatory confrontation. The Oxford orientalist R. C. Zaehner, whose formalism is not always matched by his tolerance, has remarked that experience, when divorced from dogma, often leads to absurd and wholly irrational excesses. Those of us who have been devoting our lives to the study of consciousness have been able to collect considerable sociological data about the tendency of the rational mind to spin out its own interpretations.

I advance the hypothesis that those aspects of the psychedelic experience which subjects report to be ineffable and ecstatically religious involve a direct awareness of the energy processes which physicists and biochemists and physiologists and neurologists and psychologists and psychiatrists measure.

I am treading here on very tricky ground. When we read reports of LSD subjects, we are doubly limited. First, they can only speak in the vocabulary they know, and for the most part they do not possess the lexicon and training of energy scientists. Second, we researchers find only

Researchers find only what they are prepared to find. what we are prepared to look for, and too often we think in crude psychological jargon concepts: moods, emotions, value judgments, diagnostic categories, social pejoratives, religious clichés.

–The Politics of Ecstasy

5
TAKING ACID
WITH PRISONERS

When we were at Harvard we were fortu-
nate enough to have wonderful coaches, people like Aldous Huxley and Alan Watts. There
was a crazy Englishman named Michael Hollingshead
who had a very mischievous sense of humor. His brain
was so addled with mystical experiences that he saw life
as the cosmic chuckle. He was my assistant at one time;
we were trying to test the ability of psychedelic drugs to
change people's behavior. So we
went to a prison because that's
the obvious place where you can
measure change: whether they go
back and commit more crimes, or
whether they stay out of prison.

We were taking LSD and similar drugs with maximum-security
prisoners who were all volunteers.
We explained what we were doing. We weren't doing anything *to*
them; we were doing it *with* them.
We would take LSD with them in
the prison. The first time we did

Aldous Huxley

It seemed like the most scary, reckless, insane thing we could do: to be going out of our minds in a maximum-security prison with the most dangerous, evil, homicidal people in the world!

it, it seemed like the most scary, reckless, insane thing we could do: to be going out of our minds in a maximum-security prison with the most dangerous, evil, homicidal people in the world!

We got to a moment in one of the first sessions when we were all looking at each other. We psychologists were afraid of the prisoners because obviously they were dangerous maniacs, and they were afraid of us because we were crazy scientists. Suddenly we were looking at each other, and they said, "What's happening?" and I said, "Well, I'm afraid of you," and they all laughed, "Well, we're afraid of you," so then we just broke up in laughter.

For the next two years the entire prison experiment continued—which was very scientific; we had personality tests, controls, and the usual procedures—but basically everyone who was involved in it knew it was a big escape plot. We were trying to help them get out of prison. We would get them paroled, and in general help them get going in life. It seemed so simple to rehabilitate prisoners, rather than make it into a crime-and-punishment saga of grand-opera criminality. That was an experiment which did in fact cut down the prisoners' recidivism rate in Concord, Massachusetts, about 75 percent.

Good Friday

We worked with about thirty Divinity students. We had several professors from the Harvard Divinity School, famous ministers, and the dean of the Boston University Chapel involved. It was on a Good Friday, and we gave half of the Divinity students psilocybin mushrooms (the other half didn't take them) to see if they indeed had mystical experiences. It developed into an incredibly wonderful, warm, funny mystical experience in which in the most lighthearted way we were helping people get beyond the confines of the church and the ritual.

What a Trip!

When we got back home after working in the prison, we were exultant: *What a trip!* Here we were, taking these wild drugs inside a prison, while the criminal-justice officials were all cheering us on! Meanwhile we were seeing the comedy of life and the foolishness of repetitious behavior and having a good chuckle.

The same thing was true after the Divinity School project. It started out so solemn and so serious with the hymn singing and the dean of the chapel giving sermons, and it ended with a tremendously life-affirming sense of joyous laughter. We got back to my house and were drinking beer afterward, feeling that we had tested ourselves, and tested human nature, and tested the extreme limits of the nervous system in a way that would seem almost unbelievable. We were taking "dangerous" drugs in a prison or giving "dangerous" drugs to Divinity Students with the top professors from Harvard, the Newton Seminary, and Boston University and it all turned out to be a human coming-together!

> It started out so solemn and so serious with the hymn singing and the dean of the chapel giving sermons, and it ended with a tremendously life-affirming sense of joyous laughter.

–As told to Andrea Juno in an interview for RE/Search #11:
Pranks!, 1987, from *Chaos & Cyber Culture*

IN DEALING WITH PSYCHOCHEMICALS, THE ONLY THINGS WE HAVE TO FEAR ARE ANCIENT ENEMIES—IGNORANCE AND PANIC.

–*The Politics of PsychoPharmacology*

The Redemptive Agent

Terrestrial Techologicans always endowed the Great Redemptive Agents—Buddha, Christ, Krishna—with supernatural and other-worldly powers that separate them in time and potency from the Hive Reality. "Supernatural" is jargon to describe anything beyond Hive-Platitude.

Pre-Fabricate the Future

The task for Evolutionary Agents is to pre-fabricate the future, to build new hives, to custom make Plan-Its, to teach scientific mastery of the nervous system as an instrument to decode atomic, molecular and sub-nuclear processes so as to attain immortality, cloning, and extraterritorial existence.

—Intelligence Agents

6

JOHNNY ACID-SEED

Most of the time at Millbrook, after sorting through all the Buddhist and Hindu philosophies—some of which could get pretty tedious, pretty solemn, and pretty moralistic, we tended to end up with a Sufi approach, in which there was that light touch, and a sense that if you take enlightenment too seriously, then you've pulled it down. It's got to have a bounce or a joyous movement and a smile on it.

Richard Alpert was my partner at Harvard. He came from a wealthy New England family; his father was the president of the New York/New Haven/Hartford railroad. Richard had his own private plane.

We would fly around the country in his Cessna, basically dosing people. One morning we left New York and flew down to Duke University in North Carolina, where Dr. Joseph B. Rhine, the world's leading authority on extrasensory perception, had kept his parapsychology laboratory going for years.

We Turned On Dr. Rhine

Rhine was a Harvard graduate. His main problem was that he was so intent on proving that it was scientific that it was impossible for anything telepathic to happen!

There was a sense of real basic healthiness and openness about what we were doing. We simply couldn't make any mistakes, because our hearts were in the right places.

He was using cards, and sorting, and using the rituals of highly experimental contrived psychology. But at least he was still gung ho. He'd been studying parapsychology for twenty years, and nothing much had happened; he needed all the help he could get.

I'd originally met Rhine a bit earlier, when he came to Harvard and gave a lecture. It was the first time he'd been back in twenty years, because he'd been kicked out for parapsychology. No one on the faculty would introduce him. I did; so there was a bond of affection between us, besides the Harvard connection.

Richard and I flew down to Durham; we taxied over to the Duke University laboratory. Rhine had assembled about eight or ten of his staff to take psilocybin or mescaline or something. We sat around the laboratory where he had all these experimental devices set up. You'd be working cards or be predicting movements on graphs—they were highly structured experiments.

People took the psychedelic drug he gave, and after about a half hour he said, "Everybody line up for their assignment." It was hard to keep people disciplined. I remember that one Indian gentleman, a famous Hindu professor from Benares, a very serious, nontrivial student of parapsychology, just wandered off. Someone went with him, because we didn't want people just wandering around the Duke campus.

He wandered outside and picked a rose and came back. He handed it to Professor Rhine, and said, "This represents the ultimate in parapsychology." That's an old Hindu trick. Somehow this seemed very profound and impressive.

Soon Rhine "got the message" and called us all into his office. He sat down on the floor with his shoes off. It was the first time anyone had seen him with his shoes off—he was a "dignified professor gentlemen".

He was sitting there leaning against the wall; then he said, "Well, let's figure out where we're going to take this thing. I'm beginning to understand why we're not getting more results. We've been too..." Then he led a free-form discussion of changes in their plans that went on for about two or three hours. Then people brought in fruit juice and fruit and cheese and crackers. When Richard and I saw that everyone had been brought back to planet Earth we looked at our watches and said, "See you around!" Then we grabbed a cab and drove to the airport.

We jumped on the plane

We flew back to New York and landed at La Guardia at Butler Aviation and took a cab into New York. The New York/New Haven/Hartford railroad had a suite at the Waldorf-Astoria that Richard could use; so we walked into the hotel, ordered champagne, and laughed our heads off at the implausibility of flying down to North Carolina, turning on ten or twelve very prominent and serious-minded academicians, leaving them in a wonderful kind of creative shambles, and then jumping on the plane and coming back!

That was an example of the way Richard and I looked at each other. There was a sense of real basic healthiness and openness about what we were doing. We simply *couldn't* make any mistakes, because our hearts were in the right places. And we were watching carefully, and we would not let anybody go off on their own. There was just such an aura of youthful in-nocence—even though we were in our forties at the time—and a confidence in the goodness of human nature that during those days bad tips were almost *impossible*.

He said, "This rose represents the ultimate in para-psychology." Somehow this seemed very profound and impressive.

Richard Alpert and I were like Huckleberry Finn and Tom Sawyer going down that river having adventures with, I must say, quite pure motives.

Richard in particular always had that mischievous sense. When he became a holy man—Baba Ram Dass—he got a little preachy; a little too holy for me. He'd say, "God, I'm a Jewish boy from Newton, Massachusetts, and now I'm a holy man!" But Richard always had that twinkle in his eye and that saving grace of Jewish humour that could always bring us down to earth.

I've often compared Richard Alpert and me to Huckleberry Finn and Tom Sawyer. We were going down that river having adventures with, I must say, quite pure motives. We were not out to win the Nobel prize or to make money.

Mark Twain is one of my favorite authors of the 19th Century. There is such a mischievous quality to his wisdom. He was a very powerful philosopher. A *Connecticut Yankee in King Arthur's Court* and *Puddin' Head Wilson* with all those little twists. There is a sense of playfulness that runs all through his writings that influenced us and guided us.

A-Dosing We Went

A llen Ginsberg came to Harvard when we were very square professors, and he just laid down the whole trip to us and said, "This has been going on for centuries." He knew a lot about Buddhism, Hinduism, the beats, dharma, Kerouac, and all that; so he became our "coach". Allen and I had a deal that we were going to turn on the most influential people in New York. Allen had this thick address book, and he'd peer at it with his thick lenses and say, "Come down next weekend. I'll call Robert Lowell. Or Charles Mingus."

Richard always had a twinkle in his eye.

From *High Priest*

Allen Ginsberg

One afternoon I flew down to New York and got to Allen's tremendous, flamboyantly improverished, filthy apartment. There was something so emblematic about his disdain for middle-class values, which was very interesting for me.

We took psilocybin or something with Jack Kerouac and others. The next morning, without any sleep and with Peter Orlovkey, we took the subway and went uptown to the Hudson River westside-view apartment of Robert Lowell, and we turned him on—very cautiously, because he'd had a long history of psychotic episodes and manic-depressive flights. But anyway, Allen sat with him while Peter and I hung out with his wife. And we finished that and got him safely landed back on to planet Earth.

Then we jumped into a cab and went over to the house of Barney Rosset, who at this time had Grove Press and *Evergreen Review*. Here's a classic New York neurotic intellectual with five psychiatrists and worry, worry, worry, and with a wonderful, extremely elegant, and aesthetic apartment in Greenwich Village. We took extremely powerful mescaline . . . it was a very memorable, aesthetic experience. Most of the trip Barney was in his study worrying and complaining to Allen Ginsberg that he paid psychiatrists many dollars an hour to keep him from having visions like that! Anyway, it all worked out.

We had a philosophic laugh, just thinking what we'd done in twenty-four hours. We had turned on Jack Kerouac, and then Robert Lowell, and then the top publisher in New York.

Then it was dawn the next morning and there was snow all over New York. We left Barney Rosset's apartment. The snow had fallen on the garbage cans, everything was glistening, and the sun was coming up, and it was almost impossible to tear our eyes away from the blanket of magic that covered the squalor of New York.

Finally we got back to Allen's apartment and had another one of those philosophic laughs, just thinking what we'd done in twenty-four hours. We had turned on Jack Kerouac, and then Robert Lowell, and then the top publisher in New York. It took courage and it took confidence in ourselves and knowledge of the yogic process to do this. And when it was all over, we looked back at what we had done, and could hardly believe we had performed these implausible acts.

—As told to Andrea Juno in an interview for RE/Search #11:
Pranks!, 1987, from *Chaos & Cyber Culture*

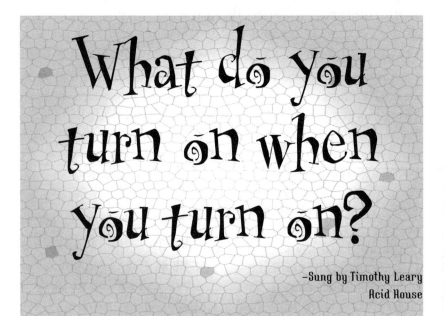

What do you turn on when you turn on?

—Sung by Timothy Leary
Acid House

Boot Up Your Brain

The human brain—the most complex, infinitely and imaginatively complex knowledge system—has a hundred billion neurons, and each neuron has the knowledge-processing capacity of a powerful computer. The human brain has more connections than there are atoms in the universe. It has taken us thousands of years to even realize that we don't understand the chaoties of this complexity. The human brain can process more than a hundred million signals a second and counting.

The human brain can process more than a hundred million signals a second and counting.

The best way to understand the evolution of the human race is in terms of how well we have learned to operate our brain. If you think about it, we're basically brains. Our bodies are here to move our brains around. Our bodies are equipped with all kinds of sensory inputs and output ports to bring information into the neurocomputer. In just the last few decades, our species has multiplied the ability to use our brains by a few thousandfold.

The way to understand how efficiently you're using your brain is to clock it in rpm realities per minute. Just on the basis of input/output, my brain is now operating at a hundred times more rpm than it did in 1960.

When we were back in the caves a million or so years ago, we were just learning to chip stones to make crude tools. We lived on

Behind your forehead you carry around a 100 billion-cell bio-electric computer that emits realities. –Intelligence Agents

a planet where everything was natural. There was almost nothing artificial or even handmade—but we had the same brains. Each of our ancient ancestors carried around an enormously complex brain that eventually fissioned the atom, sent human beings to the Moon, and created rock video. Long ago we had the same brains, but we weren't using our abilities. If the brain is like a computer, then the trick is to know how to format your brain—to set up operating systems to run your brain.

Our bodies are here to move our brains around.

Once you've formatted your brain, trained your brain with that method, you have to go through that program to use it. The process of formatting your brain is called imprinting. Imprinting is a multimedia input of data. For a baby, it's the warmth of the mother, the softness, the sound, the taste of the breast. That's called booting up or formatting. Now baby's brain is hooked to Mama and then of course from Mama to Daddy, food, etc., but it's the Mama file that's the first imprint.

There is the ability to boot up or add new directories. To activate the brain is called yogic or psychedelic. To transmit what's in the brain is cybernetic. The brain, we are told by neurologists, has between seventy and a hundred buttons known as receptor sites that can imprint different circuits. Certain biochemical (usually botanical) products activate those particular parts of the brain.

—Chaos & Cyber Culture

Why stay in an unfriendly reality tunnel?

7

CLOUDS GATHERING

As soon as we stepped outside the
science game, academics didn't know how to react.
Faculty members were increasingly concerned that
our research was "unscientific". Walking in on a Swami
clad in a loincloth doing a headstand on the conference
table didn't help matters.

Colleagues were concerned by our unorthodox experiments and views. Huxley, in particular, disapproved. He
thought that my approach to LSD was a disguise for my
game of resisting authority. It seemed that he, and others, thought that I'd transitioned from Harvard professor
to a kind of psychedelic Johnny Appleseed cultist. Others
called me a pied-piper.

Well-meaning colleagues urged us to work within the
system. They argued that administration of drugs had
been assigned to the medical profession for healing disease. Don't be foolish, they warned. Our non-medical use
and dispensing of drugs made us dope fiends. Play ball
with the system. Follow Freud's example and co-opt the
medical profession.

We ignored this "good" advice because intelligent use
of psychedelic drugs required a new profession, unfamiliar
to the western world: the brain guide—the multiple-reality
coach. We set out to fill that void.

Howard Hallis, from *High Priest*

In the early days Dick and I enjoyed the most
wonderful bond: a loving brotherhood, a Sun-
dance-Butch Cassidy alliance of psychological
outlaws working to market and merchandise
expanded consciousness.

–Flashbacks

Political Troubles

The seeds of our political troubles with other faculty were sewn during the initial meeting of the group, when we decided to make our research existential-transactional. Our experiments would not follow the medical model of giving drugs to others and then observing only external results. We would teach ourselves how to use the drugs, how to run sessions. **You have to go** Since we were using a new kind of micro- **out of your mind** scope, one that made visible an extraordi- **to use your head.** nary range of new perceptions, our first task was to develop experimental manuals on how to focus the new tools. The scientists we trained could then use the drugs precisely and safely, on themselves and others, to study any and all aspects of psychology, aesthetics, philosophy, religion and so on.

One day in a faculty meeting Dr. Herbert Kelman lead the charge in voicing the faculty's worries and annoyances with our research. We were called unscientific, accused of engaging in irresponsible research, and corrupting student morality. They appointed a committee to oversee our research. We knew that the end was coming soon.

With ever more students begging to participate in our research and ever more parents complained Harvard was increasingly uneasy. A kind of LSD black market had grown up around the campus. It was not an image that Harvard appreciated. When, in May of 1963, college authorities discovered that undergraduates had experienced our powerful entheogens Dick and I were dismissed from Harvard. I was fired for not showing up to my classes and Dick was fired for giving psilocybin to an undergraduate in an off campus apartment.

Undaunted, we organized a privately financed research group called the International Foundation for Internal Freedom (IFIF). The idea was that, provided they met mental health standards, anyone could request a guided LSD trip. We set up a psychedelic study center—a summer camp—in Zihuatanejo, Mexico, but before we could resume full-scale LSD sessions, the Mexican government stepped in, and, anticipating adverse popular reaction, demanded that we leave the country.

I had become the messiah and the martyr of the psychedelic movement.

Fortunately Lady Luck was looking favorably on us when we found the 64-room gothic mansion with 3200 acres at Millbrook. The Hitchocks who had substantial trust funds had just purchased the property. Susan Hitchcock was a strong supporter of our research. They turned it over to us to use as a commune and base of operations. We were welcome new comers to the nearby small town until the stories began to filter out and they realized that the place was occupied by a bunch of freaks.

For three years I promoted "drugless" seminars but it was too late. The genie was out of the bottle. LSD had taken on a life of its own. We were about to enter the Summer of Love when LSD burst forth to the world. Of course, life at Millbrook was not at all drugless. We continually experimented with "imprinting" **Change your** new "reality tunnels". Eradicate old mental **mind as often** conditioning and change your mind as often **as possible.** as possible. Reality is what you make it.

–Information from *Flashbacks* and other writings about Timothy Leary.

8

MiLLBROOK

Millbrook was a very special moment in modern history. We had 3,200 acres on an incredible estate where a mad Bavarian millionaire had built castles, drawbridges, gatehouses, and extraordinarily architected forests, shrines, hidden lakes, and secret groves. It was like a Tolkienian situation where we were almost totally protected, being in the middle of a 3200-acre realm. It was very difficult for law enforcement, or anyone, to get to us.

We were on our own property minding our own business yet the whole adventure was mind-boggling and scary to those people who wanted to see it that way. For about five years we used this

Millbrook—a special moment in time.

Peter Gould (from *Psychedelic Prayers* by Timothy Leary)

wonderful geographic base station as a place to explore human consciousness and the far antipodes of the human brain.

Change Was Constant

We kept changing the script. I've talked to many people who were there for a week or a month and they would say it was like *this*. But actually it would change each month. A teacher of Gurdjieff would come along and for many weeks we would study, live out and try to imprint the ceremonies and the notions of that particular approach. Then some crazy vegetarians would show up and we'd all go on nonprotein diets for a while. There was an openness to change, to experiment, and to innovate. Usually once a week there would be

Riding bareback and barefoot

a psychedelic experience; someone would guide it. That person could design it; choosing the music, the rituals, the aesthetics, the schedule . . . taking people on *trips*.

There was a sense of adventure and a sense of exclusion. There was always a sense of playfulness because we felt that what we were dong was the most innocent and the most idealistic—ultra-romantic in a way—based on books like Hesse's *Journey to the East* and *Mouny Analogue* by Rene Daumal: the classic stories of epic adventures of the mind.

ANYTHING THAT DESTROYS BUREAUCRACY ENHANCES EVOLUTION.

–Intelligence Agents

So on the outside what we were doing might have seemed very dangerous to society and threatening to police, but it actually was a very innocent sort of adventuring.

Mischievous Humor

During the heightened suggestibility of an LSD experience, this mad Englishman, Michael Hollingshead, solemnly everyone that there was a mysterious cave or tunnel under the castle where we could confront "the wisest person in the world."

He had everyone hold burning candies. With dilated eyes and spinning heads, people followed him down into the basement, which was kind of old and dark. And then, with the torches burning, he lead us down into a tunnel where we had to crawl under the foundation of the house, holding our candles. We crawled through various passageways, then suddenly come around a corner where the mischievous prankster Hollingshead had put a mirror! That was the ultimate confrontation with the wisest person in the world! Some people got freaked out by that, but ...

Persian Initiation

There was a professor from Princeton who was a lifetime student of Persian mystical poetry. He had done a great deal of translating. He wrote us, and then came up and visited. He said, "Obviously, most of the translations into English are wrong, e.g., that famous line from the *Rubaiyat,* 'a loaf of bread, a jug of wine, and thou.' The Islamic people don't drink wine. The original Persian signified hashish." But this word was not in the vocabulary of people like Edward Fitzgerald and other Oxford dons who were translating Persian poetry into some kind of Scoutmaster Upper High Anglican prose. Having dedicated his life to the study of this mystical state, yet never having *experienced* it, this Princeton professor was eager to have us provide an "initiation" for him.

So we set up an LSD experience for him in the enormous baronial "living room" of this castle we lived in,
which boasted high arched ceilings and a fireplace that
could hold twenty people. We transformed this room into
the motif of a Persian paradise, bringing in mattresses that
we covered with silken tapestries. On the walls we hung
Sufi paintings and embroidered wall hangings, and scattered Persian artifacts about. The whole room was lit with
Aladdin's lamps. The music playing was Persian music
and Sufi chants, some of which he had provided.

Time of His Life

The professor was having the time of his life—his
eyes were closed, and he was chanting along, and so forth.
Then three of the young women of the staff came dancing
into the room wearing belly-dance costumes. They were
carrying trays of fruit, fine wine, and beautiful cutlery. It
was the most elegant kind of presentation—not bawdy in
any sense; it was just as though they had walked right out
of the canvas of that famous Haroun at Raschid painting. I
know that when I looked up, I couldn't believe it either—
but the amazed professor from Princeton felt he had defi-
nitely gone into Allah's realm!

Incidentally, apparently there are some sections in the
Koran that describe heaven where Allah lives as being this
kind of situation; so we were literally making heaven come
true! At first the professor was quite stunned, but he transitioned smoothly into the program, and enjoyed it.

–As told to Andrea Juno in an interview for RE/Search
#11: Pranks!, 1987, from *Chaos & Cyber Culture.*

REMEMBER SET AND SETTING: THE BETTER
THE PREPARATION, THE MORE ECSTATIC
AND REVELATORY THE SESSION.

–*Your Brain Is God*

Start Your
OWN RELIGION

Gather your friends together and start your own religion. The Temple, of course, is your body. Your minds write the theology. And the holy spirit emanates from that infinitely mysterious intersection between your brain and the brains of your team.

Search your very own genetic memory banks, the Old Testaments of your DNA-RNA, past incarnations, and Jungian archetypes. Choose your own Gods to be smart, compassionate, cute and even goofy, if you want.

When your behavior and consciousness get hooked to a routine sequence of external actions, you become a dead robot. Just like I was a dead robot, computing back and forth to Kaiser. This period of robotization is called the Kali Yoga, the Age of Strife. This relentless law of death, life, change (DLS→LSD) is the rhythm of the galaxies and the seasons, the rhythm of the seed. It never stops.

–Turn On Tune In Drop Out

Steer your own course!

It is time to die and be reborn.

Illustration by John Thompson, reprinted from *The Illuminati Papers*

Tim, the Crazy Wisdom Guru

It is time to drop out, to turn on, to tune in.

Drop Out

Detach yourself from the external social drama, which is as dehydrated and ersatz as TV.

Turn On

Find a sacrament which returns you to the temple of God, your own body. Go out of your mind. Get high.

Tune In

Be reborn. Drop back in to express it. Start a new sequence of behavior that reflects your vision. But the sequence must continue. You cannot stand still.

DEATH. LIFE. STRUCTURE.

D. L. S. D. L. S. D.

—Turn On Tune In Drop Out

How to Turn On

To turn on is to detach
from the rigid addictive focus
on the fake-prop TV studio set
and to refocus on the natural
energies within the body.

To turn on, you go out of your mind and...

1. Come to your senses—focus on
   sensory energies.

2. Resurrect your body—focus on
   somatic energies.

3. Drift down cellular memory tracks
   beyond the body's space-time—
   focus on cellular energies.

4. Decode the genetic code.

—Start Your Own Religion

Prayer

Prayer is the compass, the gyroscope for centering and stillness. Prayer is ecstatic communication with your inner navigational computer. You can not pray to an external power—that is begging.

To turn on, you must learn how to pray.

Conventional prayers, for the most part, have degenerated into parrot rituals, slogans, mimicked verbalizations, appeals for game help. But when the ecstatic cry is called for, you must be ready to address Higher Intelligence. You must be ready to pray. When you have lost the need to address the Higher Intelligence, you are a dead man in a world of dead symbols.

–Start Your Own Religion

Turning on is a compleX, demanding, frightening, confusing process. It requires diligent yoga.

—*Start Your Own Religion*

To turn on, you need a sacrament.

Sacraments

A sacrament is a visible external thing that turns the key to the inner doors. A sacrament that works is dangerous to the establishment that runs the fake-prop TV studio—and to that part of your mind that is hooked to the studio game.

Today the sacrament is LSD. New sacraments are coming along. Sacraments wear out. They become part of the social TV-studio game.

Elements of social control do not readily understand the use of an active sacrament, such as that probably used by Socrates, Plato, Aristotle the Roman Emperor Marcus Aurelius and other famous Greek and Romans in the Eleusinian mystery religious rites during the Classical Ages.

−Start Your Own Religion

Full-Time
PHiLOSOPHER

Alan Watts gave us a model of the gentle-man-philosopher who belonged to no bureaucracy or academic institution. He was a wandering independent sage, supporting himself with the immediate fruits of his plentiful brain.

—*Flashbacks*

Watts was a full time philosopher.

Rick Griffin from *Chaos & Cyber Culture*

The Summer of Love was launched January 14, 1967 with the
Human Be-In and ended October 6, 1967 with the Death of the
Hippie march, a mock funeral staged in the Haight-Ashbury.

Change Your Brain!

Reimprint.

Create a new reality.

—Change Your Brain

The Fifth Freedom

We rejected Huxley's elitist perspective on who should have access to entheogens and adopted the American egalitarian open-to-the-public approach. It was a critical fork in the road. The Fifth Freedom is the right to manage your own nervous system. We all should have access to mind-expanding drugs. Our Grand Plan was to train influential Americans in consciousness expansion. They would help us generate a wave of public opinion to support massive research programs, licensed procedures, training centers in the intelligent use of drugs.

The Fifth Freedom is the right to manage your own nervous system.

We started plotting a "neurological revolution", moving beyond scientific detachment to social activism. We would no longer be psychologists collecting data. We would create data.

We reasoned that wars, class conflicts, racial tensions, economic exploitation, religious strife, ignorance, and prejudice are all caused by narrow social conditioning. Political problems are manifestations of psychological problems, which at bottom seemed to be neurological-hormonal-chemical. Positive social change occurs when we can help people plug into the empathy circuits of the brain.

> You are the manager
> of your destiny.
>
> –The Politics of Self-Determination

Two Commandments

The fifth freedom wasn't just a free ride wherein anyone could do *anything*. There were two basic rules or Commandments:

I. Thou shalt not alter the consciousness of
   other persons.

II. Thou shalt not prevent other persons from
    altering their own consciousness.

These commandments are not new. They are specifications
of the first Mosaic law—that man shall not act as God to
others. Be God to yourself, if you can, but do not impose
your divinity on others. They are also specifications of the
two Christian commandments—thou shalt love God and
they fellow person.

There are several obvious qualifications of the first commandment. Do not alter the consciousness of your fellow
person by symbolic, electrical, chemical, molecular means.
If the person wants you to? Yes. You can help others alter
their consciousness. Or you can get their conscious-altered
permission to alter their consciousness—for them in the
direction they want.

There are several obvious qualifications of the second
commandment. The first commandment constrains us
from preventing others from altering their consciousness
by means of symbols. This is the familiar "freedom of ex-
pression" issue. But now we must not prevent others from
altering their own consciousness
by chemical, electrical or molecular
means. These are new freedoms
which the wise men who wrote
the American Constitution and the
People's Rights did not anticipate,
but which they certainly would have included if they had
known.

**We would no longer
be psychologists
collecting data. We
would create data.**

Can you prevent others from altering their own consciousness if they thereby pose a threat to others or to the
harmonious development of society? Yes. But be careful.
You walk near a precarious precipice. Whenever society
restricts the freedom of human beings to alter their own
consciousness—by means of symbols or chemicals—the
burden of proof as to danger to others must be on society.
We can prevent others from doing things which restrict our
consciousness—but the justification must be clear.

–The Politics of Ecstasy

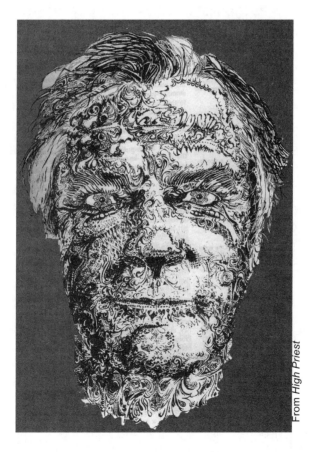

From *High Priest*

Be God to yourself, if you can, but do not impose
your divinity on others.

Post-Heisenberg Determinacy Principle

This principle seemed to eliminate any hope of objectivity. A philosophic angst, a sense of scientific futility, was the first reaction to Heisenberg's dictum. "Alas," the Newtonians groaned, "we can never really know what God or Nature hath wrought, because, the very act of investigating changes the situation."

The very act of investigating changes the situation.

We have now matured enough as an intelligent species to realize that Heisenberg's Principle is, in actuality one of Self-Actualized Determinacy. We now understand that everything we see and know is a function of our reality-mapping, i.e., a function of the way we program our brains. Let us call this the Principle of Neurological Determinacy. And with the Self-confidence, courage and freedom thus attained, let us accept the responsibility implied.

Yes, within the limits of our genetic stage we shall responsibly determine—construct, create, fabricate— the new realities we inhabit!

—Intelligence Agents

CONSTRUCT A NEW REALITY TODAY!

PHILOSOPHERS ARE AD-MEN

I asked **Marshal McLuhan** for advice about how we could dispel the fear surrounding psychedelic drugs. Instead of the horrors described in the media, psychedelics should be associated with beauty, glamour, sexuality—and personal freedom.

In *Flashbacks*, my "official" autobiography, I explained how McLuhan's insight had a profound impact on how I presented myself after that. Battles in courtrooms are not going to win much ground he explained. "Tim, you call yourself a philosopher, a reformer. Fine. But the key to your work is advertising. To dispel fear you must use your public image. You are the basic product endorser. Whenever you are photographed, smile. Wave reassuringly. Radiate courage. Never complain or appear angry. It's okay to come across as flamboyant and eccentric. You're a professor, after all. But a confident attitude is the best advertising. Become known for your smile."

I would always smile and never frown or act the victim.

I resolved to become a living advertisement for the joy, happiness and wisdom that LSD could bring. I would always smile and never frown or look the victim. Even when handcuffed and surrounded by police, I would smile. And I did. -*Information from Flashbacks*

I BECAME AN AD-MAN

Philosophers create new models of the universe.

To be successful philosophers must sell large numbers of people on their new models. Successful philosophers are advertisers.*

—*Flashbacks*

*I unveiled my slogan, "Turn On, Tune In, Drop Out!" at the Human Be-In on January 14, 1967, which lives on today, sometimes as "Turn On, Tune In, Boot Up!" as well as other variations shamelessly eXappropriated by ad-men of Madison Avenue.

CIA Funded Research

A Harvard psychologist who fought to remove Timothy Leary and his cohorts from the University faculty in 1963 was among researchers who received funds from a CIA program that sponsored drug research even more controversial than theirs.

Dr. Herbert Kelman, Harvard's Richard Clarke Cabot professor of social ethics, acknowledged having received a grant from the Human Ecology Fund, but said that he didn't know at the time that **Always know who you are selling out to!** the organization served as a conduit for CIA money. It's important to always know who is buying you.

Kelman said he requested and received funds for non-drug-related purposes in 1960—three years before he successfully argued for Leary's expulsion and that of co-researcher Dr. Richard Alpert for their alleged use of Harvard undergraduates in LSD research.

It came out years later that the CIA had established the Society for the Investigations of Human Ecology, also known as the Human Ecology Fund, as part of its multimillion dollar program on mind control and human behavior designated MK-ULTRA.

It is little known that the Ecology Fund sponsored work similar to Leary's during the 1950s at the Massachusetts Mental Health Center in Boston, and that students from Harvard and other area universities were reportedly used as subjects in those experiments. Leary informed his subjects, whereas the CIA admitted giving reality-altering drugs to unknowing persons. They violated the First Commandment: Thou shalt not alter the consciousness of other persons.

– The Boston Globe, "CIA Funded Research by Opponent of Leary," by Al Larkin, Sept. 1, 1977, from Intelligence Agents.

The performing philosopher
does not come down the mountain
with truths carved in stone.

The philosopher comes to bat several times a day, trying to whack out a conceptual hit. In baseball, a batter who gets one hit out of three will usually lead the league.

A thought-inventor is voted into the Hall of Fame or wins the coveted MVP—Most Valuable Philosopher—award on the basis of batting average over the years. For example, one-third of my ideas are kinda silly; one-third are kinda boring; but one-third are home runs.

When those ideas enter your brain they can impregnate, fuse with your other thoughts and create software for programming your life.

–*Intelligence Agents*

Most Valuable Philosopher

9
i Fought the Law*

My first run in with the law came on December 20, 1965. Rosemary, the kids and I were on the way to Mexico for Christmas but we were turned away at the border because of my previous problems in Zihuatanejo. On our way back to the U.S. checking station Rosemary realized that she had a little pot in her tiny silver box. She should have tossed it, but instead Susan hid the little box in her underwear. Bad idea.

Officials recognized me and, even though we had not actually entered Mexico, they gave us the full treatment. Our luggage was thoroughly searched and, incredibly, we were stripped to the buff for a cavity search. They found the silver box.

I was naive!

I wanted to shield Rosemary and the kids if I could. I stepped up to the plate and took full responsibility. I was charged with smuggling and transporting narcotics and failing to pay the tax on the contraband—even though we had not crossed any border.

*and the law won!

"They want to make an example of you," the guard said in a hushed voice. I wasn't going to submit passively to the role of scapegoat, the Harvard psychologist who got in trouble over drugs. Liberty was at stake

here, freedom of access to my own body and brain; a right
I believed was protected under the Constitution.

Sitting in the dark prison cell, I was filled with self-righ-
teous indignation about the wickedness of the marijuana
laws. I resolved to fight my case in the courts, to mobilize
legal teams, to devise courtroom tactics, to file appeals,
motions, briefs, depositions, to speak in defense of my
right and the right of all American citizens to manage our
own bodies and brains.

Make an example of me they did.

I was sentenced to 30 years in jail and fined $40,000. I met
with civil liberties lawyers. The federal marijuana law had
been slipped through Congress as a tax statute in 1927.
My case argued that it was a stark violation of the Fifth
Amendment because complying with the marijuana law
required self-incrimination. The general consensus was
that the law would be thrown out when my case reached
the Supreme Court. Passing a new anti-grass law would
involve hearings giving us the opportunity to demonstrate
that pot is not a narcotic. We were convinced that decrimi-
nalization was inevitable. Like I said, I was naive.

Harassment at Millbrook

Four months after the Larado incident in April of 1966 I
was the target of further harassment by the authorities. Late
one night a squad of Dutchess County police, with G. Gordon
Liddy leading the charge, descended on Millbrook, searching
it from top to bottom, to find a minute quantity of marijuana.
I was lead away in handcuffs along with confiscated plant
material that subsequent lab testing revealed was peat moss.
If convicted I could have been sent to prison for 16 years.

Rosemary spent a month in jail for contempt when she
refused to cooperate. The harassment was unrelenting.
Helicopters buzzed the estate. Police stopped our guests and

ticketed them for trivial things like dirty windshields. If they couldn't put me in jail, they intended to run me out of town. They succeeded. Billie Hitchcock had enough of the scandals and booted us out of Millbrook in the Spring of 1968.

LSD Made Illegal

Spurred on by stories of psychedelic psychoses and dire warnings of instant insanity, the LSD controversy escalated along with my notoriety. Two Senate subcommittees conducted widely publicized public hearings on LSD. My testimony while being questioned by Teddy Kennedy can be found in *The Politics of PsychoPharmacology*. Soon three states—California, Nevada and New Jersey—enacted laws prohibiting LSD illicit use, possession, distribution and manufacture. On October 6, 1966, LSD was made illegal and all legal scientific research programs on the drug in the U.S.A. were shut down. Many heads noted the parallel between the hellish ruling and 666, the sign of the beast.

We Won!

On 19 May 1969 the Supreme Court (*Leary v. United States*) concurred with me and declared The Marijuana Tax Act unconstitutional. My 1965 conviction was quashed. The state could not expect a citizen to declare possession of an illegal substance in order to pay tax, they ruled, because doing so would be self-incrimination.

My freedom was short lived. In December Rosemary Jack and I were sitting in a car in Laguna Beach when we were approached by Officer Neal Purcell. He made no secret of his dislike of freaks and longhairs. Purcell smelled the pot when I rolled down the window. Probable cause. Searching the car he found two roaches in the ashtray. When the forensic team vacuumed my pockets they found seven old flakes of marijuana.

Law of Ju-Jitsu: The more energy that is directed against me, the more energy available for me.   *-Your Brain Is God*

Mainstream political parties were no fun at all. I was determined to make my party fun to join! When my campaign became an actual threat they put me back in jail.

Official Campaign Poster from *High Priest*

It was a great day! I announced my candidacy to run against Ronald Reagan for Governor of California. My campaign slogan was "Come together", join the party. We would rent a railroad car and travel around the state with the greatest musicians and counterculture heroes.

Rosemary and I joined John Lennon and Yoko Ono in June 1969 at their Montreal "Bed-In". Lennon wrote my campaign song, *Come Together.*

–The Politics of PsychoPharmacology

Threw the Book at Me

I didn't contest the case in court so I was denied bail and Rosemary got off with a suspended sentence; Jack with 90 days. I was sent to Houston to be re-tried on the old Larado bust. Even though I'd not crossed the border I convicted of smuggling and sentenced to 10 years. Then I taken back to California where I got a second 10-year sentence for the Laguna Beach arrest—*not* to run concurrently. It was clearly a politically motivated sentence.

I was naïve. The judicial process has never been favorable to philosophers. Look at what happened to Socrates. Would I choose this arena of battle again? I don't know. It was a stage that I had to go through. And go through it I did.

I was beginning to enjoy the fray and no longer regretted being an outcast. And I was not alone.

The judicial process has never been favorable to philosophers.

Millions of Americans were beginning to openly resist the drug laws. A cultural revolution was brewing.

–Information from *Flashbacks* and other writings about Timothy Leary.

Question Authority

Think for Yourself

–Timothy Leary's website.

Look at What Happened to Socrates

Socrates has been considered by many as the greatest philosophers, even possibly an enlightened being akin to Christ, Buddha, Krishna or Mohammed, Socrates is credited as being the father and fountainhead of philosophy and ethics or moral philosophy,

Socrates believed wisdom sprung from an awareness of one's ignorance. He knew that he knew nothing; all error came out of ignorance. Socrates urged his students to focus on self-development and not on accumulating possessions. Socrates said that "ideals belong in a world that only the wise man can understand" making philosophers people suitable to govern others.

Leaders of Athens were angered by Socrates views, accusing him of being anti-democratic and of corrupting youth. Neither charge demanded the death sentence, yet he was convicted and sentenced to death—for his ideas. Interestingly, more jurors voted to condemn Socrates to death than those who initially voted to convict him. So it seems that many jurors who believed Socrates was innocent condemned him to death anyway. You see, hive dynamics at work!   –Channeled by Tim

HOW TO
iNCREASE iNTELLiGENCE

*A*ccording to Aleister Crowley there are three ways to increase your intelligence:

1. Continually expand the scope, source, intensity of the information you receive.

2. Constantly revise your reality maps, and seek new metaphors about the future to understand what's happening now.

3. Develop external networks for increasing intelligence. In particular, spend all your time with people as smart or smarter than you. We assume that you are the Intelligence Agent from your gene-pool, so you will seek Intelligence Agents from gene-pools who will stimulate you to get smarter. *—Intelligence Agents*

$$I^2$$

This planet may have been deliberately seeded with DNA by some cosmic Johnny Appleseed.

—Intelligence Agents

Fear of Newness

*I*t was hard for us to understand, in 1962, how any open-minded person could oppose the planful accessing of altered states of consciousness. Granted that the field was new and the avalanche of new data confusing, the parallels to the discovery of the microscope and telescope were so obvious that we were naively unprepared for the instinctive revulsion expressed by so many intelligent, distinguished scientists at the notion of brain change. Alan Watts, always the wry student of history, never tired of reminding us that Vatican astronomers consistently refused to look through Galileo's telescopes.

Our initial romantic idealism was soon sobered by the realization that there are powerful genetic mechanisms, reinforced by society, geared to react with fear at the approach of the new. This neophobia obviously has survival value. At every stage of evolution each gene pool has been protected by those with nervous systems wired to cry *Danger! Caution!*

> Neophobia obviously has a survival value.

The evolutionist urging change says, "There is nothing to fear except fear itself." The survivalist replies, "There is everything to fear except fear itself." At most periods of human history those who promote fear have been in ascendance. When we examine every other form of life, we see that a nervous, jumpy animal alertness to danger is a constant preoccupation.

After innovation forces of caution, reason, tradition reimpose fear to preserve what the change-agents have created.

At certain times in the emergence of civilization, optimistic change-agents, believers progress, manage to push our species into new adventures. Then, inevitably, the forces caution, reason, tradition reimpose fear to preserve what the change-agents have created.

–Chaos & Cyber Culture

The First Psychlotron

A psychlotron is an environment where human behavior is intensified, accelerated, charged with high-voltage—where the social molecular structures are dissolved so that the individual's behavior and the conclusions and interactions can more easily be observed and recorded.

–The Politics of Self-Determination

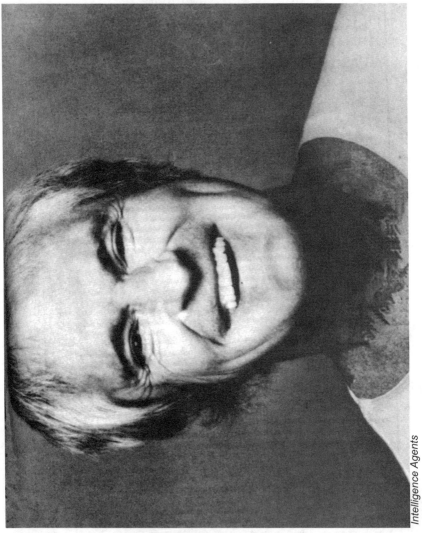

Intelligence Agents

BUDDHA, AFTER ALL, WAS ONE OF
THE FIRST DROP OUTS.

—The Politics of PsychoPharmacology

10

PROFESSOR TO

FUGITIVE PHILOSOPHER

I was sent to the California Men's Colony, a minimum
security prison near San Luis Obispo. When I arrived
in prison, I was given psychological tests used to assign
inmates to appropriate work details. Among the tests was
the "Leary Interpersonal Behavior Test"—the test that I'd
developed when at Kaiser. What a stroke of luck—or grace.

I answered the items so as to por-
tray myself as a very conforming,
conventional person with a great
interest in forestry and garden-
ing. I was hoping to get into some
kind of low security prison. It
worked! I was assigned to work
as a gardener.

**They gave me my test!
I portrayed myself
as conforming and
conventional — a
low security risk.**

On September 12, 1970 I escaped from prison by shim-
ming along a cable that stretched to a phone pole outside
the prison wall. The Weathermen took me to a safe house
where Rosemary was waiting. For a fee paid by The
Brotherhood of Eternal Love, the Weathermen promised to
smuggle us out of the country to Europe.

The feeling that I had made a nonviolent escape was a sense of tremendous exaltation and humour and joy. I laughed and laughed and laughed, thinking about what the guards were doing now. They were going to discover my absence, and then they'd phone Sacramento. Heads would be rolling. The bureaucracy would be in a stew.

This kept me laughing for two or three weeks. I felt it had been a very successful piece of performance art. Providing an example, a model of how to deal with the criminal-justice system and the police bureaucracies. Nonviolent theatre. We all thought that this was a great joke—one never appreciated by law-enforcement.

Disguise.

I imagined being recognized and hearing the clink of handcuffs. They would be expecting me to paste on a beard or moustache. Surveillance of international flights was at an all time high. Could I really get by sharp-eyed security guards checking each face for hijackers—and fugitive philosophers?

"They won't be looking for a balding businessman," Kelly chuckled. "Get ready for the barber. Get your shirt off and sit." She trimmed my hair into an American Legion butch, snipping close to the scalp at the top of my head. "Now to shave the top," she grinned as she squirted lather on my head and draped it in a hot rag.

A balding stranger peered out of the mirror at me. I gasped at how I'd change. I began to feel a little reassured. Rosemary laughed deeply.

Holding a new passport a bland-looking, middle-aged man walked through the metal detector onto the TWA flight to Paris. Across the aisle I caught the eye of a pleasant-looking young woman featuring a bubble perm, and winked.

Off to Algeria

We arrived in Paris and a week later I flew to Algeria in September 1970. I was looking for Eldridge Cleaver, a fellow exile, who was staying at the Black Panther's Amer-

SOUL ON ICE
by Eldridge Cleaver
Introduction by Maxwell Geismar

"A spiritual and intellectual autobiography that stands at the exact resonant center of the new Negro writing... a book for which we have to make room—but not on the shelves we have already built."   *Richard Gilman, THE NEW REPUBLIC*

ican Embassy—a luxurious villa. Cleaver and other members of the Black Panther Party had offered us asylum and protection. The Panthers had been recognized by the socialist-Islamic Algerians as the American government in exile when they fled the U.S. after a 1968 shoot out with policemen in Oakland.

Things went well at first—until we tripped. Rosemary had smuggled in Orange Sunshine acid and my friend Stew Alpert had brought in a delegation of hippy activists. Eldridge liked acid when he tripped with Jerry Rubin and Abby Hoffman. Our trip together was not so successful. Set and setting. Dropping acid in a revolutionary camp. Cleaver brooded most of the time, lost in paranoia.

I lost favor with the Panthers. Cleaver placed us under house arrest, claiming that I had become a danger to myself and to my hosts because of my appetite for LSD and sex, which he said was counterproductive to bringing about true revolutionary change.

Cleaver frightened us because he was very dictatorial. The Panthers were increasingly threatening, holding us in a dirty room for three days. The situation was touchy. We had to escape again.

-Information from *Flashbacks* and other writings about Timothy Leary

—*Intelligence Agents*

Timothy of Arabia

THOROUGH-BRED RACE RESULTS

Oh, it's no matter who sires them.

And it's no matter who trains them.

And it matters not who rules them
by the Reign.

Racers will only go as fast and as far and as
high as they are bred to go.

WIN, PLACE, SHOW

The (human) race is One by a Head.

Infiltrate the future!

—Intelligence Agents

11

A ONE PERSON COUNTRY

it was December 1971 and I had become a Fugitive Philosopher scrimping along on Five Brains in the Swiss Alps where I had been extended political asylum. I was aimlessly spinning gears. My broadcast-energies were low. I was the uneasy guest of a local Valaisan, who attributed his difference from other Swiss to laundered descendence from Carthaginians who had passed along the great Rhine History Highway that runs from Geneva to San Bernardo. I was unaware that my landlords were milk-fed pink-cheeked Arabs and that my host and partner, Michel Hauchard, was an arms dealer. He said that he had an "obligation as a gentleman to protect philosophers", but I suspect that he mostly had a book deal in mind.

My chalet was a cozy museum of Valaisan culture with six-foot-high cuckoo clock, large stone-carved fireplace and crossed swords on the wall. Michel Hauchard had arranged matters with the realtor and the owner who both dug the money and the glamour of housing a bona fide exile fugitive philosopher sponsored by a gangster.

Not much was happening at Crans except natives taking money from middle-class Italian skiers—an old Carthaginian custom. So I was pushed into the vacuum as village celebrity. It was a familiar role.

Protective Eye of Swiss Security

On the 27th day of December Michel called. He was agitated. "Ah Teem, I have just been talking to the Chief of Police here. He has just received word from Bern....

"About my political asylum?" I asked.

"No. That will come soon, But today the police tell me that threats have been made against your life," Michel continued.

"I don't believe it," I said emphatically.

"Well the police are worried. They want to talk to you this afternoon. You must come to Lausanne," Michel said.

I pointed my car down the twisting road from Crans at a tight, strong speed, curving along the shoulders of the hills. It is a lonely drive. The stone-walled, timber-roofed farmhouses were stuck on the slopes, each seeking a view of the valley below. The neat Calvin peak of a church tower appeared and disappeared as the road wound down to the Rhine highway, then west past Martigny to Aigle, nestled at the end of Leman, past the damp jailhouse gloom of Chateau Chillon to Michel's penthouse.

Michel piloted the Rolls up the cobblestone hills of Lausanne to the cantonal Department of Justice guarded behind stone fortress walls. The Chief of Police was genial. He thanked Michel for the watch and happily discussed the size of ski boots Michel was to buy for his wife. They were interviewed by a plain-clothed inspec-

tor who chatted with Michel about Napoleonic history.
"Do you think these anonymous phone threats are serious?" asked Michel.

"We don't know. We have reports from Algeria that Eldridge Cleaver claims he is keeping the Professor under surveillance. Maoist groups in Paris and West Germany have announced that he is a threat to the Armed Revolution because he depoliticizes young people. The Israelis want to swap him for a few jets. Arab militants view him with sympathy as an American fugitive. What do you think?" asked the Inspector.

"I think the whole thing is a hoax," I said.

"Privately," confided the Inspector, "1 am inclined to agree. However, I have been instructed to offer you a full-time bodyguard if you wish it,"

"Male or female?" said Michel.

"Not at all," I exclaimed in alarm, thinking of the threat to my eroding life-style.

"I thought so," smiled the Inspector slyly. "At any rate you need not worry. Twenty-four hours a day you are under the protective eye of Swiss security."

Extradition Rejected

"Congratulations, mon vieux," gushed Michel Hauchard. "I have just received word from Benvoglio. The Swiss government has rejected the American request to extradite you."

"The congratulations go to you, mon voyaguer," I answered.

"Listen, Benvoglio says he is besieged by reporters and television people wanting an interview," Michel continued.

"I think I should remain quiet. Doesn't he?" said the Fugitive.

"I agree. But le maitre wants you to come to his office this afternoon. I think his desire for publicity may be outweighing the need for discretion."

"What should I do?" I asked.

"It's a small moment of triumph. It's the first time Switzerland has turned down an American request for extradition on political grounds. This has implications for the Swiss drug policy. The Swiss Foreign Office told reporters that twenty years in prison didn't seem reasonable punishment for two half-smoked butts of marijuana in the ash tray of a car which was not registered to you. Not bad, eh? Maybe we start a hashish import company. And the political significance! Up until now Switzerland has regularly given refuge to fugitives fleeing west from communism or socialism. This is the first time the Swiss have opened the front door."

"But why hold a press conference? To whom do we want to signal?" I asked, beginning to wonder what I was getting into.

"It will be good publicity for our book, Teem." Michel pressed on, "I can't tell you over the phone how much money all this has cost us. Several cabinet meetings about your case. And the pressure from the White House? It's not every day that John Mitchell comes to Europe to chase a fugitive. We had to pay a fortune for this so we might as well ride the wave while we have it. I'll have the French press pick it up. You make some talk in French, eh?"

Swarms of reporters were waiting for the Fugitive in Bern. Sizing the situation up with one glance, I walked across the street and stood in front of a restaurant appropriately named "Exil". And thus was taken the famous "Exile photos" which were flashed out on planetary wire-service.

The press conference took place in Benvoglio's office. The lawyer waddled around wreathed in smiles. The Swiss Bar Association was strict about publicity-seeking so the advent of a notorious client was welcome.

I enjoyed talking to the sympathetic hip-haired English and American reporters. I delivered a brief speech in French thanking the Swiss people for their tradition of liberty.

After the reporters left, I posed the question to Maitre Benvoglio: "What about asylum?"

What About Asylum?

"Hmph. Yes, of course," snorted the lawyer. "As you know, the Federal government cannot give you asylum. Switzerland is a Confederation of very independent states. Only the canton can give you permanent residence. Monsieur Hauchard tells me he is negotiating with the Canton of Vaud to take you. I am also planning to contact other countries. I have talked to embassy people from Denmark, Sweden, Holland and they are going to consult their governments. You are in an interesting position. Ordinarily it is not difficult to locate a stateless person. But in your case, the American government will put pressure on any country that accepts you. You would not believe the pressure they put on our foreign office. And from the White House it comes."

"I'm not surprised," replied the Fugitive Professor. "There is a former District Attorney named G. Gordon Liddy who made a name for himself by harassing me. He's become an influential member of the Cultural Police operating out of the White House. I'll have to remain in exile as long as the present administration is in power. I'd like to stay in Switzerland if a canton will accept me."

The lawyer continued, "It is a matter of diplomacy. You must think of yourself as a one-person country. And I shall act as your ambassador at large. You are like Israel in 1948. The more countries that say they will accept you, the stronger your position here. Then the pressure on the Swiss government will be lessened. Our government is not eager to make anger from America. Your application for asylum will be presented to the cabinets of Denmark and Holland in the next few weeks. After that I get you admitted to the United Nations. I do my best for you. And a bit more."

THE BODY IS A PLEASURE INSTRUMENT.

—Intelligence Agents

12

SPEED IS THE CHALLENGE

Back in Crans, the Scandalous Fugitive was becoming addicted to skiing. Early mornings I strapped on my skis by the front door of the chalet, skied down to a rope-lift which ascended to town, lumbered through the village and cable cars up to the spectacular view of the high plateau, fifty miles down the Rhine valley. High, wide and clear.

> *Ski-Town Sociology*: The smart natives run the cash registers. The solid natives keep the lift machinery running and collect tickets. The stocky, tanned instructors smile knowingly. The Latin-American propeller-set ski and dance. The colony of American-Canadian ski-hippies work, ski, and fuck. There is no shortage of instructors.

> *Neurological Note:* The first step in skiing involves rewiring the Second Circuit of the Nervous System—sensory kinesthetic, hooking up newly-discovered muscles, total attention to bicep mechanics, re-mastering balance, learning new asanas, plough, christie, stem christie, parallel.

My guru was Craig, a blond kid from Oregon. He was a Yale graduate and a leading figure in the snow commune just down the slope from my chalet where twelve young snow-pilgrims shared expenses, worked four hours, skied four hours and stayed high in front of the fire dancing, listening to music, talking philosophy and fucking.

Instructor Craig came by the chalet each morning after breakfast and we ascend together in the swaying cabin discussing Universal Questions.

Craig, a mountain climber, infected me with peak-madness. He wanted to teach me skiing in the winter and climbing in the summer.

Diary Entry: The skiing goes slowly. Recapitulation of evolution: the first problem for the beginner is the struggle against gravity, to remain erect on long plastic boards attached to the feet. Craig patiently slides ahead shouting instructions for an hour and then, in relief dives headlong down the slope. For the expert, gravity being no longer a problem, but an asset, the challenge is speed.

Skiing is a mating ritual of the technological young. Families show up for weekends and vacations, but the numerical majority and the neurological charge is sexual. It is a sport for the courageous, virile, healthy. My slipping, straining attempts leave me an admiring anthropological mammal clinging to the slippery slopes of evolution.

The Faster You Go

I strained through novice exercises for three weeks. At the beginning my muscles were weak from unaccustomed movements. I was on the slopes from ten until five every day, but progress was slow. For fifty years my gross musculature had been programmed to deal with the pull of gravity without swinging my hips.

I watched the Swiss three-year-olds, brought to the slopes on weekends by parents. Sliding along with confidence, being trained to ski at the time when nervous systems are most vulnerable to learning anti-gravity maneuvers.

After three weeks of straining I apparently sensed that the time had come to re-imprint. After loosening my conditioned patterns and suspending imprints by means of Neurological Techniques developed in the research laboratories at Harvard University, I found himself standing on skis at slope top, brain disconnected from body and laryngeal muscles of the mind. Bathing, as it were, in Waves of Energy.

Craig, standing next to me, waved and plummeted down the slope. Without hesitation, I opened the door to my body, climbed in, turned the dial and followed, imitating every movement of my guru. Freed from mind and habit, the Body is a simple vehicle to operate. One points the skis downhill and slides the contours of the slope. The terrain does the thinking. Slight changes in direction are accomplished by shifting my weight and swinging my mid-section.

Freed from mind and habit, the Body is a simple vehicle to operate.

The faster you go, the more control you have and the easier to maneuver! There is little to do except surf the swift gravity wave. To make sharp turns you skid both skis until they point in the new direction. But this must be done at the highest possible speed. Slowing down is yielding control to gravity's grasp.

Craig, glancing back, saw his wild-eyed pupil, laughed, and kept going. We soared down the expert slope, miles of curving, twisting descent, and skid in a shower of snow at the bottom.

Craig lifted his poles in exultation. "You have broken through. You can ski."

"It is a moment of Neurological Revelation," I shouted. "Like the First Fuck." I motioned to the lift-bar. Once again. Faster. I couldn't wait to get to the summit. Standing on the crest I shouted my discovery. "The faster you go the safer you are!"

I pulled back the sleeve of my jacket to check my watch. "Let's time it. Faster."

For the next two hours the Fugitive rode his body down the run, marveling at rushing pleasure—like the first acid experience. High speed philosophy. All-out kinesthetic yoga.

Before cracking this hedonic gap, skiing, like adolescent sex, had been inefficient groping work. Two minutes to descend twenty feet, straining, pushing skis against slippery snow, leaning on poles, anxiously studying each yard of surface, struggling to keep control, to go slow. Total larval concentration on which muscles to be pulled, which angle to be wrestled. The satisfaction came in remaining erect, unharmed.

The faster you go the safer you are!

Now I flashed through two kilometers in two minutes. Ice patches, formerly terrors to be avoided were now accelerators to be shot through. Moguls were now round energy clusters to be used as turn curves. What had been feared was now used to increase intensity and control. The snow-covered mountain was an anti-gravity energy-apparatus bristling with knobby dials to select, direct, modulate, amplify the wind-swift current.

Neurological Yoga

The sun had set. Craig and the Professor stood at the summit looking down at the Rhine valley and the orange clouds. There were no other skiers left, only the restaurant staff bundling into the last cable car down. The wind whipped the unprotected peak.

"I hate to leave," he said.

"We're always the last ones to come down," I nodded in agreement.

We plunged down the right side of the valley wall, skid around the left turn throwing up waves of snow, dove straight to the base of the high T-bar lift, veered right, bumping through the steep mogul field, threaded down the narrow, icy roadway, slashed a sudden right-angle down a wide, steep meadow, slid right again, burst under the tow cable out to the top of the mid-slope, and raced, hunching low, poles tucked under armpits, wind ripping our faces.

At the bottom station we reached down to snap off bindings, swung skis over shoulder and, suddenly earthbound, clumsily rolled in ski-boot, high-gravity gait along the village streets to the saloon. We stacked the skis outside and opened the door to a rush of warm air scented with alcohol, smoke, perfume and the steam of healthy bodies. The atmosphere had that soft-electricity of congenial, happy, sophisticated people who like themselves and each other.

Intelligence Agents

We order beers and sit back, content. "It's addictive." I pronounced. Craig smiled in agreement. "It's neurological yoga. It's muscular meditation. It does everything that the oriental gurus claim, but it's more.

"The danger bit is fascinating," said the Philosopher. "The risk buzz."

"Power freed for pleasure and clean speed," said Craig. "I'm glad you got the hit today.

"It's happened for you and you can never lose it. It's very sexual." I motioned to the saloon filled with hi-fi people. "It's new, you know, like a mutation. High speed skiing has just developed in the last twenty years. It's part of what's happening all around. Electronics and computers and jet planes and space travel. It's the same principle and it's the exact opposite of what we learned in the old life. It's the paradox of technological civilization. The faster you go the more control you have. Like the pilot flying 700 miles per hour with finger-tip control. On the ground you need a tow-tractor to make the plane turn."

"You go up and you come down," Craig inserted.

"And a lot can happen up there. Sometimes you don't come down with whom you went up. You move with those at the same velocity," I philosophized.

–Intelligence Agents

The body is the car; the nervous system is the driver.

–Musings on Human Metamorphoses

13

PRESSING SEX AND DANGER BUTTONS

Craig and I slid off the T-bar at the restaurant door, kicked off our skis, stacked them in the rack, and ambled up metal stairs to the restaurant, our faces glowing with sunny mountain vigor.

My espionage eye immediately picked up two acquaintances in the crowded restaurant. Our photographer, camera strung around his neck, was waving hello. The fugitive's emergency circuits flash warning. I was legal but incognito in Switzerland. Michel had warned me that the police can protect me from extradition from the country but not from expulsion from a canton. I knew that if there were too much publicity, Mastronardi could not head-off the Swiss xenophobic, right-wing politicians.

The other signal came from the corner of the restaurant where our beautiful black-haired associate sat beaming a Hormonal Invitation. I stopped in my tracks and received her Mating and Rapture messages. The multi-buzz pressed my Sex and Danger Buttons. I was programmed to believe that Risk is the eternal concomitant of the fully utilized brain.

Sharon Hennessey Knoop from *Intelligence Agents*

Discovering the body as an instrument of
freedom and pleasure is like finding out
that a car can be used for pleasure driving.

–*Musings on Human Metamorphoses*

"Who is the slim Sophia Loren?" I wondered aloud.

"I don't know her name," said Craig. "She hangs out with the Latin-chic set. I've seen her dancing at the clubs."

"With whom is she sitting?" I asked.

"They're rich Mexicans, spoiled sons of the Mexico City aristocracy. The short one with a mustache, Pedro, his father owns a big newspaper. The tall, good-looking dude, his family is a big industrialist. They go to European schools and hang around the smart spots. They ski like matadors. Weird macho scene. The females don't ski at all. They come up on the cable cars and spend the day here in the restaurant chattering and fluttering and giggling and playing card games, shrieking, Uno! Dos! Tres! Cuatro!"

"You don't seem to like your Southern cousins," I observed.

"They just don't make it here. Socially I mean. The Brazilians and Venezuelans do. They hang out at Gstaad and St. Moritz. Their women have more class. Play backgammon and ski and conduct adulteries with finesse. But the Mexicans strut around getting into barroom brawls. The South Americans are European, really. But the Mexicans seem to have a peasant morality. Machismo. That girl isn't Mexican. I could never figure out why she runs with them. She's got a different style."

"Let's go over and find out. Who is the photographer?" I wondered.

"He's from a local paper down in the valley," replied Craig. "He's cool. Smokes grass. Likes the Stones. Is that enough to pass his security check?"

I walked across the restaurant, waving the photographer to follow. The beauty smiled and made room for me to sit next to her.

She called herself Maria and said she was Brazilian. We arranged to meet that night at Le Sporting.

The club was her turf. Males lined up along the bar, waved and blew kisses as she passed by. Feeling every bit the Fugitive Doctor, I was charged with sparkling South American energy and danced with dervish smoothness.

Later, she came back to the chalet and threw my hashish in the fire. "I can make you feel better than that," she said with passion. I gave her a tantric art book. For two nights we played at seduction and then she classically took me as Her Lover.

Sexual Flower

During the week Maria modeled in Lausanne. Weekends she was the Perfect Mistress—elegant, bawdy, funny. Her translucent skin was a lavender-pink, Andalusian enamel. Her tawny corazon basket was opal on smoky gold, admirably adapted to the rounded contour of the hand. Her contessa-face was etched crystal, eyes in dark enamel. She spoke no English, luckily. So we fused in basic French. Her gestures were gitane-erotic, like Rita Hayworth. To say Espagnolade is not to be overly derisive.

One afternoon while performing some lazy yoga I puts a small crumb of Kabul resin in her mouth and said, "Mangez. It will relax your muscles."

The neurograms look like a Cannabis Rapture Commercial. "Oh mon amour, jamais, jamais," she murmured. Her

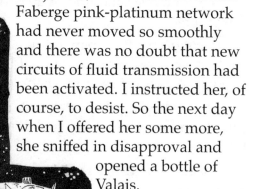

Faberge pink-platinum network had never moved so smoothly and there was no doubt that new circuits of fluid transmission had been activated. I instructed her, of course, to desist. So the next day when I offered her some more, she sniffed in disapproval and opened a bottle of Valais.

Pete Von Sholly from *The Game of Life.*

She was programmed to do anything for Her Lover. Passion, fervor, ardor, fever, desire, longing, yearning.

She was crown jewel of Terrestrial Domestication, Princess of Ceremonial Linkage for whom Kings put aside Thrones, Ambassadors forget their duties, Maharajas carpet marbled floors with rubies. She was programmed to do anything for Her Lover. Passion, fervor, ardor, fever, desire, longing, yearning. "J'aime pour deux," she murmured, eager to suffer, mourn, lament, languish, anguish, pine, grieve, despair. She loved to dance, flirt, fuck, tease, coquet, vamp, lick, excite, titillate. She was the perfect racy drunk, a joking Shady Lady, dancing down to Rio, cooking gourmet meals, laughing in ways none of Her friends would believe. I worshiped her as The Sexual Triumph of Feudal Civilization, but when I looked aloft on starry nights I was lonely.

Maria and skiing are what was happening before I was ejected from the Canton of Valais.

—Intelligence Agents

Auto-mobile!
Joy-ride your body.

—Musings on Human Metamorphoses

Triumph
of the Hippies

*A*n interesting thing happened when the first post-war baby boom generation of mutants hit college in the 1960s. I suspect that on every womb planet like ours, one generation after Hiroshima, you get a wild, volatile hippy-dippy all-out neural-change movement. Each gene-pool senses that a quantum jump into the future is about to happen, a retooling for a model change and each gene-hive squirts out its new experimental models. On this nursery planet these new models were called Hippies.

So, let's consider the 1960s. I think it's important, as we rocket into the 21st century, to understand what happened back then because there is a tendency to sweep that decade under the rug. Few people understand what happened between 1960 and 1970. I am here to remind you that the global

Bill Ogden from *Psychedelic Prayers*

neurogenetic revolution of the 1960s was the most important decade in human history.

Fellow veterans from the uncivil war of the 1960s, you

The 1960s was an important decade that launched a wave of change that swept every aspect of American and global culture.

gentle shock-troops won a noble victory for DNA. Let me remind you how you changed every aspect of American and global culture in the 1960s. Your mutational signal reached and shook-up every gene-pool and hive-bureaucracy on the planet. You may suspect I am biased because I was a genetic activist in the 1960s.

But let me confess to you I have not one nostalgic bone in my body. I am certainly not here, my fellow veterans, to lead a Charge of the Haight Brigade back to Woodstock. We shall salvage, not sentimentalize the past. As we move into the future we shall take the best of the 1960s with us. You must not let Them at hive-control turn you into vegetating veterans like the American Legion and the VFW. Or seduce you into annual conventions at places like Philadelphia where you wear funny costumes and run around barefoot and get busted for old times sake.

I make gentle fun of the 1960s, but I am serious when I say that this was an important decade. There is not one gene-pool in the American hive that hasn't been re-formed because of the 1960s.

YOUR BRAIN CREATES YOUR OWN REALITY.

–Intelligence Agents

Individual Freedom

History, indeed, evolution itself, can be chart-ed in terms of the growth of Freedom-of-the-Individual.

Freedom is

1. Amount of **mobility**—velocity-altitude, and communication-scope attained by the individual.

2. Amount of **direction-control** of transportation-communication attained by the individual.

3. The **opportunity** of free-responsible individuals **to** signal each other and **link-up** in more complex networks inevitably leading to migration.

Question Authority

Individual freedom is the key to evolution

14

MAGICAL MYSTERY TOUR
OF SWITZERLAND

Sergius Golowin, a Swiss historian and member of the Bernese Legislature, lived between the lungs at Interlaken. His arcane specialty was the magical, occult, Celtic thread of Swiss history. During my exile Sergius took me around to the sacred shrines of the Confederation. We visited the Witches Meadow, the enchanted valley of Brother Nicolas, the charmed Celtic forest high in the Lycergic Alps and the cave of the Irish hermit above Interlaken.

Sergius, as though in a dream or trance, would escort me to a carefully selected site, read from a history book about the events that occurred there, strike a pose and have his picture taken with me. I later discovered that Golowin was re-enacting scenes from ancient paintings, re-living the visits of former philosophers as if re-making old Celtic Reality Mov-

Sergius Golowin

ies. I got the strong impression that I could not leave Switzerland until I had traced the steps of the Celtic migrants who had passed through the High Valleys on the voyage to the western lobes.

Visiting Paracelsus

One day we drove in his yellow Porsche to Einsenin, south of Zurich, to visit the birthplace of Paracelsus. We carved through pastoral beauty that hip Swiss in their boredom call their country— the Green Hell—past meadows and tidy farms, into a small village where, amazingly, there rose a medieval cathedral, towering, expansive, fronted by a broad St. Peter's cobblestone plaza where three hundred thousand pilgrims used to assemble from all over Europe.

Inside it was dark, heavy oppressive, high, solid like the cathedral of Sevilla. In the enormous mausoleum there were so few people walking like ants. Old women dressed in black. In the scone floor under the central dome was a circle, fifty feet wide, of mosaic designs. As journey-men, Intelligence Agents always look for secret keys that open to higher levels, Sergius and I picked up Brotherhood of Masons vibes. Secret psychedelic cult-spoor.

Sergius Golowin

The game was to look for the hidden message. In the cathedral of Einsenin, once center of European Christianity, there is a large circle of the twelve astrological signs hidden by the pews. They are so large and scattered that only a time-traveler would notice. Astrology, with its evolutionary and caste implications, was one of the dangerous drugs of the Middle Ages. How did they get away

Astrology, with its evolutionary and caste implications, was one of the dangerous drugs of the Middle Ages.

with embossing pagan symbols in a Catholic Cathedral? Maybe the Zodiac was so suppressed that the local inquisition didn't know the details of the heresy.

We returned to the car and drove past neighboring convents and seminary dormitories out along a country road overlooking the lake, down a side road and across a bridge. Sergius was an impressive navigator, but he did get vague in the fine tuning. He knew the house of Paracelsus was just beyond a bridge. He asked at the nearest farmhouse and came back with the information. Everything in sight had belonged to the family of Paracelsus.

We walked down a path to a high vantage spot and thought about the great alchemist who played here as a boy before wandering around Europe, teaching, studying, experimenting, getting arrested, and deported from Basel, hiding from the Bernese police, seeking asylum in Prague—home of alchemists. He was the father of modern chemistry, and modern medicine. Jung claimed him as founder of dynamic psychology. Basically he was an alchemist, dealing drugs that provided the

Paracelsus, the Alchemist

illuminated vision, the philosopher's stone which, when swallowed, tuned you into the bio-physical network and focused your neurological microscope so you could identify the web of energy. Paracelsus was the wisest and most influential mind that Europe produced, but the chemical companies in Basel don't like to talk about him too much because he was an illegal magician.

We drove back to the bridge and Sergius said "Stop!" in front of the charred debris of a burned-down house. "This is the house that was built on the site of the house of Paracelsus." We poked around the ruins. There were shards of melted glass in different colors. I stuck one in my pocket. The symbolism was asphyxiating. In front of the house, just on the other side of the bridge away from town, was a metal sign. It read: *Paracesus*. "The L is missing," said Sergius. I nodded knowingly. In this, the tidiest country in the world, the birthplace of wisest product of Swiss gene-pools was a neglected shambles.

"It's called Devil's Bridge," explained Sergius. "The Bishop who controlled the town was in charge of all road construction. Now and then dissatisfied farmers would build bridges themselves. When the agents of the Bishop went around asking who built the unauthorized bridge, they would say, 'The devil built it.'"

—Intelligence Agents

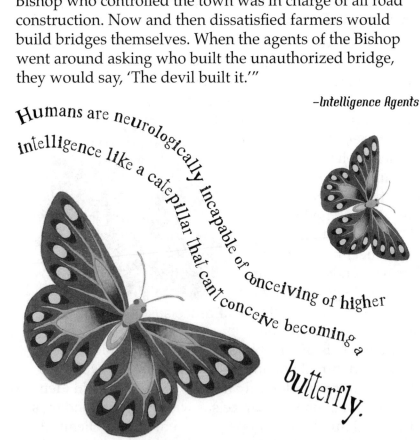

Humans are neurologically incapable of conceiving of higher intelligence like a catepillar that can't conceive becoming a butterfly.

—Musings on Human Metamorphoses

15

EXPULSION FROM CANTON VALAIS

S **ix glamour-hero-fun pictures,** along with a stir-
ring tribute from the young people of the canton hon-
ored by the presence of the Philosopher, now learning to
ski were published in a local paper. Heh! Heh! Heh!

A week later our contact on the German paper from
upper Valais published a fiery editorial accusing the lower
Valais administration of adopting the philosophy of hedo-
nism, license, and drug addiction. The headline read: *Lower
Valais Endorses Sin*.

Suddenly I became the biggest political issue since the
scandal of the bridge ten years before. The Catholic Press
(French) rose to defend me and the tradition of Swiss
tolerance. Protes-
tants denounced
Catholics. The
mountain people
on this side of the
valley were for
me. The moun-
tain people from
the other side
were vice versa.

Intelligence Agents

When someone arranged for school children to start signing petitions in my favor I knew the battle was won. The parents reacted as predicted. The two policemen who came to see me were laughing their heads off. Everyone saw what was happening and dug the controversy which would hurt no one except the foreigner.

National Party Committee took sides. The Chief of the Cantonal Police asked me down for tea. There is much "Helas," "Incroyable," "Quel horreur," but the Philosopher must leave the canton.

ZUG LAKE

The Scandalous Philosopher fled to a cottage by the Lake of Zug, under a high jagged peak called Rigi Kulm said to be the soul of Switzerland. Zug Lake was inner-schweiz, center of the Confederation—the most conservative canton, less than half a mile away the Tell Chapel perched on a hill where William shot the tyrant Gessler and initiated Swiss freedom.

My house on Zug Lake, where from the balcony I watched seven swans swim stately to be fed, was just below the hill where William Tell hid in wait for the tyrant Gessler, slew him with the extra arrow, and thus began the Swiss War for Independence. Twelve twenty-one was my phone number in the Villars Chalet. And the house on Zug Lake was in the exact center of Swiss space and time. When one moves free, Sci-Fi high above gravity pull, it's all mystic, mythic, connected overground comics.

It was harder for Maria to come for weekends, changing trains at Bern, but she did. Fantastic meetings and

Zug Lake, Swizerland

departures in the railway station. Running platform hand-
thrown kisses as the train pulled out.

Once a week I drove past Lake Lucerne, over the mountain, down to Interlaken and then up to Gstaad, where we
had established Michel for the season in a ducal chalet. He
hired a chef from Geneva but, alas, no one came to dinner
except lower-level backgammon pros and young friends
of my mistress DeeDee who made fun of me. Michel, like
Maria, was a sincere residual of the Domesticated Glamor
Morality imposed on adolescent nervous systems by the
Movie Industry of the 1940s, which (as Neuro-sociology
teaches) was ended by Einstein and Warhol. Michel was
snubbed at Gstaad by the older generation because he
failed to pay his Gin Rummy debts, and by the young because he was geared to play Playboy.

Problem of Astronautics

Maria came down with word that dinner was ready.
She had prepared trout in a white wine sauce and stood
by the kitchen door, looking like Ava Gardner circa 1950,
watching the cowboys in the saloon. She was a bit drunk.
The Philosopher, the Prince, and the slim-hipped Gambler
escorted her to the head of the table. She ate little, kept
drinking wine, then said she wanted to rest and retired to
the fireplace room. We assigned her the job of breaking up
the acid scene, but the presence of Alexis, the uncertainty
of her role in the new script, and the English dialogue
without sub-titles overloaded her circuits.

After dinner Maria sent word that she wanted to see the
Professor. She was lying on cushions near the fire gasping
for breath, just able to whisper that she needed medicine
from her bag. Brian and I searched the house diligently.
The bottle was missing.

Maria seemed to be getting weaker. I phoned a medical
friend in Basel who had no specific advice to give. Maria
refused to have a doctor called or to go to the hospital,

shaking her classic head and rolling her dark eyes, implying that she understood the course of the malaise. She looked into the my eyes and whispered solemnly, "Je vais mourir."

We men looked at each other helplessly and shrugged. Maria laid back and died. I knelt at her right and Alexis on her left. Brian Barritt's eyes bulged. Everyone in the room sensed her spirit leave her body. Alexis felt her pulse. It had stopped.

I talked to her somewhere in sky-time calling her to come back. Alexis massaged her heart. This time-travel is demanding.

From the control tower I talked to her somewhere in sky-time calling her to come back. Alexis massaged her heart. Like a plane circling for landing, her spirit touched down in her body and everyone breathed in relief.

"This time-travel is demanding," sighed Alexis. "Death-bed scenes are so Victorian. That's why we can't allow it."

Maria was lying in my arms, her black hair on my chest, her eyes closed, drifting in contented repose.

"What do you mean?" asked Brian.

"The death-bed scene is the climax of the classic Victorian drama. There the truth emerged. The achievements of medical science changed all that today. We aren't interested in listening to last words. We are concerned only that the patient live. So Maria, we apologize. We brutes would not allow you to die a heroine. We treat you, alas, like a patient," I said.

"It seemed more like a problem in astronautics to me," says Brian thoughtfully. "Who is this Maria anyway?"

The next day Maria seemed totally recovered but refused to discuss the matter.   *–Intelligence Agents*

16

GIORDANO BRUNO SCRIPT

We decided to take the cable-car up the Rigi Kulm and lunch on the summit terrace. From the peak we looked south to the four petals of Lake Lucerne and could visualize the Great Moments of Swiss history enacted below. Standing on the north parapet one looks down to the right at Lake Zug and to the left at a long green field. It appeared so close that the Prince, the slim-hipped Gambler and the Fugitive Philosopher decided to descend the cliff to the meadow and then down through the woods to the cottage.

The cliff dropped down in steep sections. A half-hour of careful footwork and jumping led to a narrow ledge which dropped twenty feet to a sheer ice slope that ended in a hundred-foot drop. A slip chutes the careless climber to slippery death. They started chopping footholds in the soft crumbling ice with sticks.

The climbers were wearing slick-soled track shoes; Brian and the Philosopher in light sweaters, Alexis was wrapped in a pink tweed coat. It was an hour before sunset. The voyagers looked at each other appraisingly. Any accident would leave them exposed all night on the mountain in the February chill. They could clamber back in retreat, but without a word spoken they decided to go ahead.

It took twenty minutes of exploration and discussion to chart the descent of the first cliff. Survival circuits were flashing alarm. The sugary foothold could crumble. A foot could slip on slushy grass-mud and body slide over precipice.

The Fugitive was scared; that is, the crisis centers of his nervous system energized neurons that control emergency glandular function. Each neuron had dozens of output fibers, each of which curled around a tiny bulb containing a chemical. When the alarm button sounded, fibers squeezed and danger drugs poured into the blood and lymph systems carrying the ominous message: Attention all units, our galaxy is in mortal danger. All-out alert. This biochemical state is felt to be most unpleasant.

Alexis, being tallest and, at the moment, the calmest, took over. He dug his way down the crevice and reached the bottom. Brian, small, wiry, cheerful, uses his foothold and quickly reached a point where he could stand on Alexis' shoulders and then drop to the level. Much against the instructions of my warning systems I followed shakily. Halfway down I felt Alexis' hand grab my ankle and moved my foot to his shoulder. When I hit safety the circuit orgasm exploded and a trillion cells receive the message: Danger alert is called off, continue normal life maintenance. The great galactic network had been mobilized for all-out survival, tested to the limit.

"The spasmodic discharge of emergency-juices," says the Wizard sitting in the snow catching his breath, "is the most basic of the 24 orgasms available to the human nervous system. The roller-coaster kick."

We stood around in the late afternoon sun smiling at each other in pleasure, like astronauts on the Ticonderoga making speeches about how proud they are to be members of the Space program, sharing post-orgasm tenderness. We started merrily down the easy grade to the right and within a hundred feet made a jolting discovery. We were trapped by another steeper cliff and this time there was no easy retreat. The sun was sinking. The neural-endocrine network began to alert for another emergency.

This time Brian led the way, a daring slice down a small crevice, reaching his hand back to steady his companions en route to another adventurous, risky, daredevil Circuit 1 orgasm, moving down the snow field to the next challenge. But the greatest dangers were still to come. Brian and Alexis explored the straight-ahead situation, seeking a path down the iceberg.

The Fugitive moved a hundred yards to the left where a stream plunged downward. Snow had collected in the stream bed and it was impossible to progress. Working slowly, chopping ice, hanging on tree limbs, he found a way down and shouted back to the others. It was hard for them to find him, hanging to the side of a narrow shelf, propped against a tree trunk. Now it is his turn to lead and they follow, Alexis slide fifty feet on the ice and bounced to his feet without so much as a crease in Brian Jones' coat.

The snow melted into a steep forest where they hang to tree trunks and slid down muddy paths. After an hour in the forest they hit the high meadow and Alexis led them running across the ridge exultant.

Night had fallen when they reach the hotel at the base camp. The tavern-bar was civilization after a long Arctic safari. The owner found it hard to believe that they had descended the dangerous west cliff of the Rig in winter! We phoned home. Maria was worried. Waiting for the pickup car they ordered beers and lifted glasses in celebratory toast.

Weeks later Brian disclosed that it had been just another Aleister Crowley tape replay. In London, North Africa, Europe, India, Egypt, the Philosopher guided by Barritt had unknowingly retraced the trail of Crowley.

"It's time you realize that you are the recipient of the brain-model which was robot-wired to play the difficult public role of Evolutionary Change Agent. You are thus being forced, one might say, by thousands of gene-pools to relive Crowley, Dr. Dee and Paracelsus," Barritt told the Fugitive.

"It's the Giordano Bruno script that worries me," I replied.

-Intelligence Agents

Beware the
Immorality Placebo

A classic ploy by which the hive stimulates stupidity is the Immorality Placebo, usually sexual or financial. In the early decades of the 21st century the PC Placebo, usually pertaining to race or sexual orientation, surpassed the Immorality Placebo in popularity with the new wave hive-bureaucrats. Interestingly, while the Immorality Placebo is favored by the so-called conservative right, the PC Placebo is the control mechanism of the so-called far left. Beware. Whether radical right totalitarianism or liberal progressive totalitarianism matters not, both are mindless hive domination. Out-Castes are not deceived.

Here's how it works: First the gene-pool sets up a Moral Taboo. Moral Taboos are magnificent Intelligence Qualification—IQ—devices because they get everyone in the hive hung up on virtue-sin. The Moral Taboo must interfere with some normal, natural caste-behavior—must perversely prevent some castes from getting something that they neurologically are wired to want. Once brought into focus by prescription the Taboo becomes charged with artificial cop-sinner magnetism.

Genesis, the first chapter in the Judeo-Christian Bible, clearly sets out the strategy of the Immorality Placebo: using good-evil as a fascinating distraction, a front, a ploy. The Immorality Placebo was formulated by Pynchon as one of his "Proverbs for Paranoids": If they can get you asking the wrong questions, they don't have to worry about answers.

If they can get you asking the wrong questions, they don't have to worry about answers.

—Thomas Pynchon
Proverbs for Paranoids

–Intelligence Agents

17

MEETING
WITH PRINCE ALEXIS

The Fugitive's hideout cottage on the lake had a fireplace study on the first floor opening onto the water. The top floor was a ship-cabin sailing down the lake; from the deck one whistled for the seven swans who floated majestically along the shore and bent strong phallic necks to swallow bread crumbs.

A London model named Pamela arrived at Michel's chalet. We suspected she was an Evolutionary Agent. She was a languorous, soporiferous nervous system transported in a slender, curved body with unbearably smooth-silk arms and skin of warm sepia enamel. Her carnelian, in the form of a snail, was surrounded by translucent red enamel pierced by a Mandrax thumb.

Before dinner, while Michel was pre- occupied instructing the chef, Pamela whis- pered to the Professor that Prince Alexis was in town and wished to arrange a meeting. He

Intelligence Agents

Prince Alexis was slim, tall, with long black hair and translucent ivory skin. He looked, if it dare be said, like a fairy story prince. He spoke Shakespearean English.

was to phone the chalet that evening. But Michel, realizing that he must prevent the meeting between Alexis and me, shut off the phone.

It turned out that Michel had fallen on such bad times that he had been censoring personal calls. The poor man signed up to play Louis XIV but all the action was going to Mick Jagger. Michel didn't like to dance, was burnt out by all-night gin-rummy, annoyed by amorous phone calls to DeeDee's nubile guests. And the Hedonists were on to his game.

So, just around midnight Pamela suggested—just like a bad girl should—that Alexis might be found at the Palace Hotel nightclub, sitting surrounded by friends, wearing a green silk shirt embroidered Psi-Phy. Roman designers dress him gratis, confided the model.

Time-Travelers Meet

Prince Alexis drove up in his Stingray, dismounted regally, threw reins to the groom and set off a three day cycle of life-death magic. Sitting in front of the fire he began to babble. The two aliens immediately recognized each other. "Welcome fellow Time-Traveler," said the Prince, "I have come many parsecs to meet you."

Prince Alexis was slim, tall, with long black hair and translucent ivory skin. He looked, if it dare be said, like a fairy story prince, holding himself with royal pride, tossing his mane in fiery petulant arrogance. Scion of a most noble family, he had been educated Everywhere and done Everything at age 25. Gossip had it that he was sexually bilingual. He spoke Shakespearean English.

"It's taken us many orbits to get here," agreed the Philosopher. "Where was your last land-fall?"

"Katmandu. Do you know Sri Ram Muni? No? Excellent. How important that I can tell you! He knows you and has sent you a message."

"That's nice," I nodded.

"I perceive," says Alexis, "a note of reserve in your voice. I share your hesitancy about Hindu swamis. I spent many months on assignment in India observing the Holyman-groupie scene. Perhaps I should explain to our lovely companions that most of the famous swamis are hip showbiz operators, campy-vampy-splashy-flashy homosexual queens with gullible followers, grand ashrams, triumphal road tours, performing restful magic. It's amusing to hear them gossip and put each other down. They follow each other's productions like jealous rockstars. Competing for the top of the cosmic charts."

"There are a few Intelligence Agents left in India," I agreed, "and they are as hard to find there as here. It's the classic paradox. The more advanced the mind, the fewer people to talk to."

"According to legend," continued Alexis, "there are sixty-four illuminated people in the world. You won't find them administering large bureaucracies. The real spiritual wizards in India don't solicit followings, don't open branch offices throughout the world, and can't be bothered with fans, groupies, bank accounts."

"What do they do?" asked Pamela, leaning her head on her shoulder and moving her silken hand up her smooth arms. "Do they dance, ski, have girlfriends, get high? Are they good lovers?"

"It is my understanding," I added, "that at least half of them are women. It is logical, isn't it, that many of them would be mated to each other?"

"You are thinking of Lama Govinda," asked the Prince.

Most of the famous swamis are hip showbiz operators, campy-vampy-splashy-flashy homosexual queens with gullible followers, grand ashrams, triumphal road tours, performing restful magic.

"And his beautiful wife Li Gomma. There's an answer to your question," I replied, turning to the Model.

"Smashing! The Holy Man and his Holy Woman," murmured Pamela. "How original. What do they do?"

Road to Almora

"They live in Almora," explained the Prince. "A small village in the foothills of the Himalayas. To reach Almora one begins with a dusty train trip north of Delhi across flat, parched semi-desert to Barelli and Katghodam. Then a bus circles up foothills, skirting gorges, crawling through dusty little hamlets where thin barefoot men in ragged clothes run alongside holding empty hands, through Nainital perched like a Swiss village by the lake and up through sad, lonely, patchy, overlumbered forests filled with melancholic Indian army troops in dark green uniforms and pencil mustaches maneuvering to exorcize the Chinese. And finally, the bus strains up to the Holy Village on the ridge, Almora.

"This is no tourist spot, you realize, way up here, two to three days travel by semi-primitive transportation from Dehli. There is not one hotel bed in Almora. The dark rooms at the inn offer a wooden frame bed with woven rope on which you throw your sleeping bag, which, if forewarned, you have ordered, custom-made with feathers and hand-sewn cotton in the teeming market of Old Dehli. There is not one concession to European culture in Almora. Not one Coca Cola, not one modern restaurant." Alexis said as he trailed off.

After a pause, he continued, "Now if you leave this outpost and climb a dirt road for two miles, past outlying villages, you come to Holyman Ridge, a high, steep wall which looks North across valleys to Himalayan Tibet, which towers above valleys to the south through which river and road to Katghodam curve downward. Scattered along two miles of the ridge, looking south, are houses in which assorted spiritual searchers, European and Indian, maintain part-time residence. The footpath then curves across the ridge and runs along the northern rim. This walkway, perhaps ten thousand years old, continues north to Tibet, and has been used by pilgrims, porters, merchants and, from time to time, warring bands. In a shack at the ridge-crossing tea has been brewed for centuries in brass pots over charcoal, served heavily sweetened in thick brass mugs."

The Lama and Li

"A mile beyond the tea shack the pilgrim leaves the main path, turns left, climbs a twisting narrow trail leading to a point at ridge-end which commands an astronaut view, North, West, and South for hundreds of miles. There, in a house built long ago by Evans Wentz, lives the Lama Govinda and his wife Li Gotama.

"The Lama can accurately be described as venerable. An old man dressed in Tibetan robes with wispy oriental beard, he is a Buddhist scholar of German descent, with an inquiring, empirical mind. Teacher, Translator, Transformer, Transcriber, Transmitter of that ancient lore passed on by a scientific elite who devote years to research. The priests and swamis are second-hand karma dealers who solace the masses with soothing rituals and pop-versions of hive ethical codes. But with Lama Govinda one talks about the laws of energy that run the universe."

Lama Govinda

Alexis had been speaking intently, not paying total attention to Pamela's Mayfair pink enamel hand on his dick or the French girl's hedonic ivory hand stroking his neck. Turning back to the Professor he appealed for confirmation.

"Isn't that what you learned in Almora?" he wondered.

"Yes," I said nodding, "Lama Govinda taught me to study the old symbol systems and to look for errors. When you find the errors and correct them, then you understand the message."

"What about Becky Thatcher?" murmured Pamela softly.

"Ah yes," continued Alexis, "the beautiful Li Gotama, Parsee by birth, performs translations, illustrates the Lama's books with graceful drawings. She adds the aesthetic half. Li means fire-light. She calls him Ch'ien, the Creative of Heaven. I fabricate that Lama and Li are two of the sixty-four illuminated people. Would you concur?" I smiled in agreement.

"The Lama and Li are your teachers," said Alexis. "But I must tell you about Sri Ram Muni. He is to be found in a small temple outside Katmandu. He has preserved certain energy manuscripts which he has decoded and wishes to pass on. He has sent me west to present the version ready for you."

The Fugitive Philosopher wrote seven digits on a piece of paper. "These are magic numbers," I said tipsily. "Dialed

into the appropriate electronic transceptor they will put you in touch with my headquarters near Lucerne. Call me and we'll continue our talk."

–Intelligence Agents

18
PRIMITIVE PSYCHIATRY

Alexis continued with his insights about India. "The fascinating facet of India," said Alexis, "is her worship of holy putrefaction. To the banal perceptions of the west she exists and has always existed, a bedraggled woolly mammoth buried in the ice of occult tradition. And yet no other ancient culture has been so expressive. In stone carving, temple, wood, gesture, fluid motion, sonorous sound, she has broadcast her buoyant message to the world. Close your eyes and sleep! Lest her repetitious dream be disturbed, she asks for only the smallest dash of creative stimulus in return. Dare we introduce western science-magic to the Ganges? Does soul, expressed in art, as in fucking, require equal reciprocity? Shall we, whether they like it or not, electrify the sita? A rock festival in Benares?"

Psychiatric Curse

"Strong cocaine," said the Professor. "Can we change the dial? Let's focus on the nearby future. What part do you want to play in our next episode?"

"What is the script?" he asked.

"That is the question. We're looking for it. The womb planet waits for our next broadcast. Unhappily it appears that we have to fabricate the treatment. What do you suggest?" I asked.

"My own obsessions are simple," replied the Prince. "Electronic rock 'n roll along the thin, aristocratic line

The professions of psychiatry are quite out of touch with reality. from Chuck Berry to the Stones. Erotic mysticism, tantra and the pursuit of that Holiest of Grails: the all-night, orgasmless fuck. Oh yes, my family history amuses me. The saga of decadence, Sybaritism, epicureanism, philosophic gratification. I am, in addition, a nervous wreck. Do you know what that means?"

"I think so," I replied with a tender smile.

"Then tell me quickly. Why?" he demanded. "Why when I talk to a psychiatrist does he straight-away want to pop me in treatment?" Alexis asked. "It's really quite unsettling. Say something, anything to exorcize this psychiatric curse."

"I'll have to make up a story," I said.

"It's all fiction," replied Alexis.

"In the 1950s," said the Professor, "I devoted nine years to the study of the personality, behavior, and strange beliefs of psychiatrists. They are a bizarre and superstitious tribe. My conclusion is that professions of psychiatry are quite out of touch with reality. Do you like that?"

"Precisely my judgment," exclaimed Alexis joyfully. "But I need more to convince me."

Nixon of Psychology

"This diagnosis does not apply to the younger generation of psychiatrists, many of whom are nice, if dull hive agents. Freud is considered by many to be a flaming revolutionary of free and honest sexuality. Nothing could be farther from the truth. Freud is the Nixon of Psychology."

"Oh that's priceless," grinned Alexis. "Freud is the Nixon of Psychology! How?"

"Every sensible person in the world," I continued, "had been trying to end the cold war, but each attempt was futile because it required someone who fanatically believed in the polarity, someone totally committed to good, to establish detente with bad. Nixon being the last politician in the world to want peace with his enemies, had to be the one to use detente against his domestic rivals. The same thing had to happen to allow a detente between Morality and Sex in the European character structure. For a century before Freud every intellectual in Europe had known about the unconscious role of sexuality. But no psychiatrist or scientist with a normal, healthy sex-life could be believed. It required the most uptight, sexless, prudish man in Europe to use sex as an ally against his real enemies, the Viennese medical establishment. Is that enough?"

"I'm a difficult case. Can you continue?" Alex smiled.

"Psychiatry," continued the Professor, "is primitive, prescientific hive regulation. Actually the pre-Freudian psychiatric language was much more realistic. Before Freud, psychiatrists were called 'alienists.' This is an extraordinarily happy term, because most psychiatric patients are aliens, that is to say, they have activated post-hive circuits of their nervous systems, circuits designed for future survival. When the UFOs land 'alienation' will become a very respectable word. The in-sane seem to live in another world. Exactly. They are perhaps best seen as premature evolutes. Mental hospitals should be called asylums. A nervous wreck is exactly that."

"It's a beautiful concept," said Alexis. "A badge of honor I shall wear proudly."

"Nervous," I explained, "refers our attention to the nervous system, not to imaginary character traits. And 'wrecked' means pushed out of normal hive alignment. Collapse of the Domesticated Mind is considered to be the goal of most mutating post-hive entities. The mind as you know, Alexis, is the fragment of the brain that mediates the movements of the nine muscles of the larynx and the hand. Collapse of the mind means that the laryngeal muscles can no longer define hive reality."   *–Intelligence Agents*

Monotheism is the primitive religion that centers human consciousness on hive authority.

–Intelligence Agents

Reality
is what
you make it.

Start **your** own religion!

–Turn On Tune In Drop Out

Eight Mysteries of Existence

The religious experience is ecstatic, jolting, wondrous, awe-struck, life-changing, mind-boggling confrontation with one or all of the eight basic mysteries of existence.

The goals of an intelligent life, according to Socrates, is to pursue the philosophic quest—to increase one's knowledge of self and world. Now there is an important division of labor involved in the philosophic search. Religion, being personal and private, cannot produce answers to the eight basic questions.

The philosopher's role is to ignite the wonder, raise the burning issues, inspire the pursuit of answers.

Science produces the ever-changing, improving answers to the haunting questions that religious wonder poses.

—Your Brain Is God

Eight Fundamental Questions

There **are eight questions** that any fair survey of our philosophic history would agree are most fundamental to our existential condition.

1. *Origins:* How, when, where did life come from and how has it evolved?
2. *Politics:* Why do humans destroy and how can we live in peace?
3. *Epistemology:* How does the mind emerge and what are our learning, information processing, communication and thinking abilities?
4. *Ethics:* Who decides what is good and right and what are our moral beliefs and rituals?
5. *Esthetics:* What is beauty and what are our modes of pleasure?
6. *Ontology:* What are our realities and how are they formed?
7. *Teleology:* How have humans evolved and where is life going?
8. *Cosmology:* What are the basic forces influencing the universe and where are they taking us?

**Philosophers ask the questions;
scientists answer them.**

–Your Brain Is God

19

AGONIZING CURSE OF PRINCE ALEXIS

Alexis gracefully rose to his feet and began to pace the floor. The flickering light from the fire painted red shadow patches on his aquiline face.

"Okay," he said, "that's enough for the psychiatric spell. Now let me present you with the more serious neurological problem. I have come eight thousand kilometers to beg of you a boon. And in return I bring you a most valuable gift."

"I am at your service," I said.

"I have fallen under a most agonizing curse," Alexis revealed quietly.

"How was this neurological imprint imposed?" I asked.

"In India. I picked up your trail, first in the ghats and ganja shops of Calcutta. Then up to Benares. And then to Almora. It's your fault really. Your visit there became a cultist legend. That's why I went there. In your footsteps I found a house on swami ridge," Alexis said.

"Not the little cottage on Snow View which looks North to the Himalayas where I stayed with the beautiful Nordic sorceress?" I asked.

"No. Near by. But I know that cottage. I stayed in a house up beyond Snow View just before the footpath crosses the ridge, " Alexis clarified.

"Just before the tea hut?" I asked.

"Yes,"" he continued. There are still many self-appointed holymen living along the ridge. Everyone who passes along the summit on the way to Lama Govinda's passes Snow View and feels your presence. Living ghosts make people nervous," he explained.

"Nervous is good," I replied. "Nerves means courage and vitality."

"Living ghosts disturb because they remind people that the mysteries are still alive. It's a scandal that you are still running around this planet upsetting hive traditions. If you were trans-migrated according to custom it would be more comfortable for everyone. You could be dealt with, commercialized, marketed, re-discovered and fed into the Messiah Biography Machine. One wave of books could

Agents must now illustrate, publicly and flamboyantly, the process of rapid, continuous metamorphosis. Change Agents continually change.

prove you a comic prophet. The next wave could demonstrate you were a shallow romantic vulgarizing the ancient gnosis. In the old linear age you would have been removed as soon as you produced a Shock. If you announce you are going to drive people out of their minds, and if you do activate them to ecstasy and terror and awe, it's the genetic duty of the Hive People to assassinate you. I find your living presence disturbing. Why do you hang around?" the Prince lamented.

"Come now, Alexis," murmured the Philosopher. "You are getting carried away with old pre-Einsteinian myths. Since 1946 the Genetic Intelligence assignments have changed. Agents must now illustrate, publicly and flamboyantly, the process of rapid, continuous metamorphosis. Change Agents continually change. Have some more wine."

I Detest the Ashram Scene

"Almora," says Alexis intensely, "still trembles with the resonance-remains of vanished Out-Castes or magicians, as they used to call them. Did you ever freak out there?"

"Of course," I laughed, "I had several splendid cosmic frights. No wonder. Siva temples, Methodist Missionaries, weird sexual cults, the underlying Hindu-Moslem antagonism, and the ominous presence of Mao across the snow peaks. If you are erotically fused, Almora is one of the highest places in the world. Were you alone there?"

"Yes," sighed the Prince. "Totally, abysmally alone."

"Tant pis. Tres dangeriuex," I exclaimed. "If you are alone, a restless, guru-seeking pilgrim or some such disconnected nonsense, Almora is a bore. People like Almora because it is a respectable bore."

Alexis sprung to his feet shouting in pleasure. He strode across the room, leaning against the wall, begin an excited speech. "Exactly. It's a small bore, low calibre, dull spiritual Eastern colony. That's how my trouble started. One night I found myself in the house of a group of people—many of whom you know. Former students, former satellites, ex-traveling companions. An old lover, beautiful but subdued."

"Well, I hate followers, disciples, imitators. I spin out through empty space hungering for stars of equal magnitude," Alexis continued. "All right, let's face it. My snobbishness was offended by these middle-class people sitting around playing instruments that they couldn't play. I'm not that good, but I have sat in with the best groups in England and—let me speak frankly—I do own the best sound equipment in Europe. So here

are these safe-and-sound people on scholarships talking Vedanta. I detest the ashram scene. YMCA tasteless.
Someone started passing acid around. I took some. Then in
disdain and irritation I seized the box and dropped around
ten pills."

"How reckless," I said in alarm. "Scornful solitude is
not the best space platform from which to launch an all-out
voyage into time."

"Precisely. Imagine my dilemma. Almora was a spiritual Disneyland. I became a mindless organism, a 20-billion
neuron network flashing a 100 million signals a second.
Moving at the speed of light. Naturally I tore off my artificial body covering," Alexis said emphatically.

"Naturally," I agreed.

"My brain sent messages to the busy little chemistry
factories in my body. Pump-pump, I squirted adrenaline
and ATP into my muscles. My strength increased one hundred percent. My naked eyes saw the lattice-fabric of reality. The energy was so great I literally glowed. Everything
was alive with electron-magnetism," Alexis continued.
And most horrible, I was surrounded by those living cores
of life encapsulated in leathery robot bodies regarding me
with distaste and fear. I was their worst nightmare come
true. I was totally freaked out."

"Fantastic," smiled the Philosopher. "Priceless."

I Ran Naked Around Holyman Ridge

"Yes, exactly, timeless and priceless. My brain
tuned into my DNA code, synapses crackling with genetic
messages. I saw with the eyes of countless ancestors. What
a rowdy band of velvet brigands I sprung from! And the
futique children to come. You understand my predica-
ment? I was a real entity from time suddenly trapped in a
fake-believe Disneyland.

The American theosophists turned away in fear. Another acid flip-out! But dig it, the Hindu natives grinned and saluted me.

Yes, that's it. I remember seeing a plastic Indian village at Disneyland with fatigued redskins selling tickets and bakelite bows and arrows to cellulose tourists. Okay, now I'm the real Crazy Horse suddenly popped down there. Whew! Quel horreur. I saw at a glance what had happened to my land and my people. I saw in microscopic despair these robots who have never felt the wild Dakota wind in their face or the taste, touch, smell, thunder sound of the living, eternal God. I screamed at them. 'Are none of you alive?' I raved around looking for another living soul," Alexis ranted.

"Yes, that does tend to happen," I commented sympathetically.

Pausing briefly, Alexis continued, "Or I was your Thomas Jefferson appearing in a modern Congress. Awake you pink-faced rubber frogs! Is this what we fought for! I was Giordano Bruno running around alive in Madame Tussand's waxworks! I was Peter, the wild-eyed Fisherman, screaming at the Jesus statues in the plaster Bibleland in Florida. Wake Brothers, let's trash this place and get back to the living soul."

Taking a deep breath, the Prince continued his rant. "Dig it, Wizard, for three hours I ran naked around Holy-Man Ridge in Almora bursting with energy, shivering in cosmic loneliness searching for a living soul. I sat in the lotus position on a rock overlooking the valley to Tibet and watched the sunrise. Good. That's all in order. I stalked regally back to the cottages looking deeply into peoples' eyes. The American theosophists turned away in fear. Another acid flip-out! But dig it, the Hindu natives grinned and saluted me," Alexis explained.

"Whew! Give me some more wine," the Prince demanded as he threw himself on his knees in front of the fire and held up his glass. The wine splashed light yellow, reflecting the firelight.

"Now, I'm getting to the hard part," he said, as he took a long sip of wine.

I nodded in understanding.

"Okay, I was loping along the road approaching the house owned by the Methodist church. Two middle-aged matron-missionaries from Kansas were standing on the steps. I loved those little ladies. They were the holiest Americans I'd found in India. So I trotted up to them in joyful anticipation. But, dig it, they both threw up their hands in some sort of defense against me. Why? Cause I was naked, I suppose," Alexis sighed.

"But I'm so pure. So as I ran by I casually swing my arms and gently, the way you'd pat a push-me, pop-up doll in the toy store, knocked each of them down," the Prince exclaimed with a mischievous chuckle.

Untouchable Psycho

"The Americans saw me tumble the old ladies. They huddled together for a Nervous Conference. I could read their minds. They were afraid my antics would jeopardize their comfortable tourist scene. If only one of them had had the courage and wisdom to groove with my energy, laugh acknowledgement and run down to the river to bathe with me," the Prince lamented.

"That sounds like the sensible thing to do," I agreed.

"Now," Alexis continued, "the leader of the American

colony was a solemn young professor of Sanskrit philosophy from Michigan State. He told me that he had been a student of yours, a humorless follower who saw you as Buddha, threw himself at your feet in worship—to your dismay I'm sure. He and his wife were visiting India on sabbatical with their two children. He notified the police."

"Oh that's too bad. Why did he do that?" I asked.

Alexis continued, "So the policeman from the village found me meditating at the Siva Temple. Do you remember it? It was like the Siva shrine in any Village with a three-foot stone carved lingam that women cover with milk and flowers. The policeman waved to me and I went along cheerfully. He popped me in a shack in the Village below the ridge and waited on guard for the Captain to come in his jeep. A large crowd of Villagers and Americans gathered around the prison shack. The Captain entered alone to talk to me.

"After twenty minutes the Captain emerged from the shack and made a stern no-nonsense speech to the crowd. He said that I was a God-intoxicated saint. He told the villagers, in Hindi, to protect me. Then he turned to the Americans. He denounced them for not taking care of their saddhus, for lacking faith in God's wisdom, for neglecting their holiest men. He spoke about the corrupting materialism of American culture and wondered why Americans bring their small-town concepts to spiritual India. He said that if they couldn't handle their saints, he would arrest, not the saints, but all of them," Alexis said in triumph.

The Prince and the Fugitive Philosopher were sitting in front of the fire, dented a bit by herb and wine. The sun was setting on the lake. Alexis had told his tale shyly.

Freak-Outs

"Is this the first time you've told this story?" I asked.

Alexis nodded. "Yes. It was my shameful freak-out. My terrible disgrace. The Americans in Almora considered me a psychic untouchable. I came halfway around the world to bare my neural wound"

"Do you want me to fabricate a helpful explanation of freak-outs?" I asked.

"Of course. That's why I told you my story," Alexis replied somewhat impatiently.

Freak-outs are created by unsympathetic, frightened people around the victim.

"Okay, let's assume that freak-outs are created by unsympathetic, frightened people around the victim. First, the nervous system retracts its imprints to hive reality and activates future circuits. Drugs can do this or it can happen naturally. When this happens you are hyper-vulnerable to signals sent by others. You don't have your laryngeal mind to grasp reality. It hits you direct. It's a nice free state but you are very suggestible. Now put yourself back in that situation. You are loping up to the ladies. If they had waved to you what would you have done?" I looked at him questioningly.

Alexis wrinkled his brow in thought. "Why, I would have waved back and trotted on. That's what happened with the Hindus."

"Good. Now, if they had fallen on their knees and prayed to you, what would you have done?" I asked.

"That's easy. I would have blessed them," quipped the Prince.

"And if they had bent over and said, 'kick me,' what would you have done?" I probed.

Nodding the Prince agreed, "Yeah, I get the message."

"What signal did they send you?" I continued.

"They crunched up in fear as though I was a dangerous maniac," the Prince answered.

"So, being in a cooperative mood, you gently obliged. Everything you did was perfect hadron particle behavior. But tell me one thing. What did you say to the Captain when he came into the shack?" I asked.

"Oh, that was easy," laughed the Prince. "As soon as he entered I murmured *Om Shiva*, threw myself at his feet and touched his boot with reverence. He was enormously pleased. Then we sat and he lectured me about God and Man and Law and Unity and Ramakrishna, and Reincarnation—standard Hindu Sunday School stuff."

EVERY INDIAN POLICEMAN HAS A YEN TO BE A SWAMI.

–Intelligence Agents

IMPRINTING IS A BIOCHEMICAL EVENT THAT SETS UP THE CHESS BOARD UPON WHICH SLOW, STEP-BY-STEP CONDITIONING TAKES PLACE.

–Change Your Brain

CHANGE YOUR
MiND Often

*T*here is no "real" reality. No constant that we
all experience. Reality is what we make it.
LSD allows us to erase our personal reality and
to imprint a new one. Why live in a reality that is
unrewarding or worse? You can choose from hundred of available realities. You are only as young
as the last time you changed your mind.

It is possible to step from one reality to another
if you learn to re-program your brain.

I CHANGE MY REALITY TUNNEL OFTEN.

–Change Your Brain

20

AN ALCHEMICAL EXPERIMENT

Everyone in the lakeside cabin was now aware of the voltage released by the introduction of Prince Alexis into the molecule. Two days in a row the Death Card flashed out of the Tarot deck.

The third night, in honor of the Prince, and by way of exorcism, we arranged an alchemical experiment which involved the dissolution of hive imprints, the transmutation of realities, the reception of vibrations from post-terrestrial consciousness.

Alexis, Brian, Liz, Barbara, Corinne and I lounged in front of the fireplace. The familiar room now so electrified that solid objects were seen to be composed of atomic and molecular bubble-chains and lattices emitting energy. A low comfortable humming sound filled the air.

After innumerable re-imprinting exercises Alexis smiled and produced from his briefcase the ancient leather text that had been sent from the Nepalese Holyman. Alexis reverently unwrapped the soft kidskin covering, unwound the silken wrap and placed the book on the carpet in front of the fire. Candles were moved to illuminate.

Holyman's Text

The book was constructed of leather panels, sewn together so as to unfold in eight sections. Alexis pointed to the Sanskrit design on the cover.

Each of the eight panels of the leather manuscript was divided into three sections and in each of the 24 panels a picture was inscribed.

"That's the number twenty-four," he said.

"Why twenty-four?" asked Brian.

Alexis smiled enigmatically and flipped open the cover. Each of the eight panels of the leather manuscript was divided into three sections and in each of the 24 panels a picture was inscribed.

The bottom panel was shaded red and contained:

1. An Amoeba with the face of a baby with huge red lips.
2. A Fish with the face of a baby.
3. A Frog with the face of a baby.

The second panel from the bottom was shaded orange and contained the pictures of:

4. A Rodent standing alertly with the face of a two-year-old human child.
5. A Lion with the face of a three-year-old child standing over and pulling a toy away from a small animal with the face of a two-year-old human child.
6. Apes swinging from a jungle-gym—with the faces of five-year-old children.

The third row, shaded yellow, contained these three pictures:

7. Paleolithic Humanoids picking up stones—they have the faces of seven year-old modern children.

8. An eight-year-old child in the body of a Neolithic—thoughtfully examining a flower.

9. Children building a treehouse together.

The fourth row, shaded green, contained:

10. Knights on horseback with the faces of teenage kids—being watched by court ladies with the faces of teenage girls.

11. A husband and wife with their children standing in front of their house.

12. A million people crowded into an enormous city square—all facing and looking up to a velvet balcony.

The fifth row, shaded a rich blue, contained:

13. A beautiful, naked, human, hermaphrodite—the body radiating energy; glowing.

14. A Yogi, naked, hermaphrodite—radiating, glowing with sense of precise control of the energy.

15. A beautiful woman and man locked in Yab-Yum position, radiating and glowing.

The sixth row, shaded light-electric blue, contained:

16. A beautiful naked human hermaphrodite. The brain is visible as are the extensive tendrils of nerves—the body glows.

17. A Yogi, naked, hermaphrodite with brain and nervous system visible—sending out tendrils of energy, which embrace and create the surrounding material forms.

18. A series of mountain tops. On each sits a Yogi with tendrils of nerve signals linking them & energizing the surrounding forms.

The seventh row, shaded violet, contained:

19. A Double-Helix—intertwined energy coils. Along the strips the preceding 18 forms are portrayed in red.
20. The Double-Helix is crowned by the head and face of a Yogi—the Yogi's Brain intertwines the Double-Helix.
21. A spaghetti tangle of Double-Helices in a spherical form—the whole image radiating like a Star.

The eighth row, shaded silver, contained:

22. Stars in a velvet Black Sky.
23. Stars which form a Galactic Brain.
24. Strips and spirals of stars infolding to a Central Black Hole.

"What does it say?" asked Brian, pointing to a script on the bottom of the scroll. Alexis pulled a piece of paper from his pocket and started reading. The candlelight shadowed his noble face. His voice was softly powerful.

"The sequence, that is, the numerical order, of evolution is everywhere the same. In the stars, in the seed, within the atom, and in the unfolding development of the individual human being.

"Having decoded the numerical sequence which governs the evolution of energy we can use this Periodic Table to decipher evolution at other levels of velocity.

"Some sequences are more easily understood in the evolution of stars. Others are more apparent in the growth and change of seed-forms. Others are most clearly seen in the growth and development of the individual human being going through the changes.

Fundamental Principles

"This parallel study of evolution in the life of stars, in the periodicity of the chemical elements, in the evolution of species on a planet, in individuals popping up at different historical epochs, demonstrates the underlying harmony and over-tone-unity of nature and helps the Intelligence Agent discover the similarities in phenomena at all levels of velocity.

"The number of basic principles which govern all processes of change is very small. Let us say there are twenty-four. Different numerical combinations of these twenty-four stages create all the seeming variety of realities which humans can receive.

"The first fundamental rhythm of the universe is polarity. This has been called "The Law of Three". This principle states that every event in the universe is the result of an intersection of three processes: The receptive, the transmitting, and the interacting process between.

"Input. Outgo. Mediated by Integration. Dendrite. Axon. And cell body. "Black Hole. Big Bang. Transition Between.

"The next fundamental rhythm of the galaxy is the Octave of Change. This has been called the law of 8 (7 + 1).

"Realities consist of vibrations. These vibrations are emitted from every form of structure along the electro-magnetic continuum, proceeding in different directions, crossing one another, colliding, strengthening, weakening one another. DNA fabricates eight brains which deal with eight evolving technologies along the energy continuum. The reason for this eight-phase spectrum can be understood only by the Six

The Law of Three
Every event in the universe is the result of an intersection of three processes: The receptive, the transmitting, and the interacting process between.

Brain Organism. There are eight (7 + 1) colors visible, eight (7 + 1) primary sounds, eight (7 + 1) is the rhythm of the chemical elements.

"Everything is in continual motion moving at fractions and multiples of the speed of light.

"The natural operational rhythm for the human nervous system is the speed of light, ever-changing. The mind of vibrations (the 6th Brain) is called the In-lightened mind. In-lightenment means thinking at the electrical rate of the Brain. The Brain is the Electrical Body. The Physical Body is the carriage for the Brain—Body Electric. Human muscular Behavior is the gross, coarse manifestation of faster, stronger nuclear vibrations—charm, charge, strangeness, attractiveness. Each impulse of consciousness from the lower neuro-muscular circuits, when received by the Electrical Body, becomes a small sun radiating meaning. The harmonizing of these innumerable units of experienced light is the skill to be learned by the Sixth Brain."

Alexis stopped reading and suddenly turned the book with both hands exposing the other side. With all the panels exposed the book was about a yard long. Each of the eight panels was a color of the spectrum.

The picture was a vague human-shape, a cloud-like figure in light blue. Within the figure and radiating were golden fibers—it resembled a surrealist anatomical diagram of the human nervous system. The light blue human figure trailed off into a network of rainbow swirls and spirals. The effect was startling. The golden-fibers of the nervous system seemed to be antennae receiving and vibrating current.

Alexis threw his head up melodramatically and held his hands out, trembling. His fingers moving as though he were palpating some invisible substance. The others could see crackling current emitting from or being gathered by his hands. He looked at me and smiled. They shifted to sit facing each other about five feet apart. I held up my hands and jumped in surprise.

Alexis, Barbara, Brian, Corrine, myself, Liz and all the objects in the room were part of a three-dimensional television holograph, in radiant color; everything constructed of vibrations that flow in fast, smooth rhythm, current alternating so swiftly that a soft texture, infinitely luxuriant, was created. All present were totally joined, indeed, were each part of the holograph, each a shifting pattern of the same field of energy. Each knew what was occurring within the consciousness of the other, could know every thought and experience that the other had ever registered. The sumptuous, voluptuous, mink-lined, rich smoothness of everything fresh, alive. The "isness" of Huxley's chair.

Alexis, Brian, Liz, Barbara, Corinne and I spend the night in telepathic wave sculpture, imprinting music, absorbing was now following me like a worshipful jealous girl, flinging a mink neckpiece over his shoulder.

"What shall we do next?" he asked.

"Find her," I answered..

"Shall I stay?" He asked.

"No. Go now. If you delay here you will be late for our next intersection," I replied.

Alexis ceremoniously presented me with the Nepalese text and left with Barbara and Corinne for Lucerne. *–Intelligence Agents*

> The objects in the room were part of a three-dimensional television holograph, in radiant color; everything constructed of vibrations that flow in fast, smooth rhythm, current alternating so swiftly that a soft texture, infinitely luxuriant, was created.

Prayer is ecstatic communication with your inner navigational system.

–Your Brain Is God

Intelligence

is the

ultimate aphrodisiac

—Intelligence Agents

The Game of Life

Eight Circuits

of Consciousness

Brian Barritt and I formulated mind maps that we called "Tongues of God" — a circuit model of consciousness where the human mind/nervous system consists of eight circuits which when activated produce eight levels of consciousness.

The human nervous system evolves sequentially through eight maturational stages. At each stage a new circuit of the nervous system emerges.

—Intelligence Agents

Nothing happens until W0men activate.

—Musings on Human Metamorphoses

Stages of Metamorphosis

Circuit	Concern
1. Bio-Survival	safety
2. Emotion-Locomotion	freedom of movement
3. Mental-Manipulation	dexterity, speech
4. Sexual-Social	parenthood/childrearing
5. Rapture	beauty, body
6. Ecstasy	reality, consciousness, neurological time
7. Neurogenetic	immortality, future of the species
8. Quantum	spirit, metaphysics, galactic time

–Intelligence Agents

LEARN TO USE YOUR HEAD.

–Musings on Human Metamorphoses

Cycles Are Evolutionary

Each of the cycles of human life involves dramatic alterations in morphology, behavior, physiology and neurological function. At each chronological stage a new imprint is taken. Each imprint determines the positive and negative foci for subsequent conditioning of the newly activated circuit. Each circuit of the nervous system has been designed by the DNA code to deal with the physical characteristics of planet earth and the corollary asymmetries of human anatomy.

Each of the stages of human metamorphosis produces a life-form that is as visibly different from the preceding and succeeding phases as the larval caterpillar is different from the metamorphosized butterfly.

Most people only access the first four circuits—the Larval Circuits—in their lifetimes. The second four circuits—the Stellar Circuits—are evolutionary and future oriented. They are equipped to encompass life in space, as well as expansion of consciousness that is necessary to make further scientific and social progress. Meditating, practicing yoga and other spiritual endeavors as well as taking psychedelic drugs helps us to shift to the latter four gears.

–Intelligence
Agents

Brainstorming The Seven Tongues of God with Brian Barritt

Intelligence Agents

THE ONLY SMART THING TO DO IS TO GET SMARTER

—Intelligence Agents

21

WRITERS
PETITION SWISS

T wenty-five prominent writers filed a petition with the Swiss government asking that it give me asylum to as a "literary refugee persecuted for my thoughts and writings" by United States authorities.

The writers—most of whom live in the Bay Area—include Allen Ginsberg, Herbert Gold, Laura Huxley, Anais Nin, Lawrence Ferlinghetti, Robert Creeley, Alan Watts, Howard Becker, Kenneth Rexroth, Michael McClure and Ken Kesey.

The eight-page petition was delivered to the Swiss consulate in San Francisco. Copies also were delivered to the U.S. Departments of Justice and State in Washington.

In New York City, playwright Arthur Miller and other literary leaders sent a cable to the Swiss Ministry of Justice in Zurich urging that Leary be given asylum "as an act of compassion".

They stated that I was a proponent of marijuana and psychedelic drugs and had fled overseas after escaping from a California prison and was being held without charges in Switzerland awaiting extradition requested by the California Department of Corrections.

Steve Gladstone (from *Politics of Ecstasy*)

Timothy Leary with Allen Ginsberg

The writers' petition cited the fact that the judge in the case, Byron K. McMillan, denied bail after describing me as "an insidious and detrimental influence on society" and "a pleasure-seeking, irresponsible Madison Avenue advocate of the free use of LSD and marijuana."

L. Kushel from *Tales of Tongue Fu*

The writers argued that I had been prosecuted for an underlying motive, "namely, essays and speeches on drug usage theory."

Government plans to put me back in prison, the petition argued, rise "merely from differences of opinion on public philosophy involving drug use, a scientific matter now being debated in professional circles."

Paul Krassner

"At stake in the case," said the petition, "… is Dr. Leary's freedom to manifest his thoughts in the form of poems, psychological commentaries, dialogues, and essays of a literary nature…."

The other persons who signed the petition were Ted Berrigan, Margo Patterson Doss, Dr. John Doss, Lewis MacAdams, Paul Krassner, Lenore Kandel, Diane di Prima, Philip Lamantia, Don Allen, Michael Aldrich, Jan Herman, Andrew Hoyem, Phillip Whalen and Gavin Arthur.

The cable to Zurich from New York was sent on behalf of the 100 American members of the International P.E.N. (Poets, Essayists, Novelists) Club. It was signed by the president of its American chapter, Thomas Fleming, by Miller, a former chapter president, and by David Dempsey, a member of the P.E.N. board.

"As American writers we are disturbed at the way Dr. Leary's writings have been cited as evidence in his trial," the cable said. It pleaded with the Swiss to give me the kind of sanctuary accorded in the past to various victims of persecution.

All Things Pass

All things pass
>   A sunrise does not last all morning

All things pass
>   A cloudburst does not last all day

All things pass
>   Nor a sunset all night

But Earth . . . sky . . . thunder . . .
>   wind . . . fire . . . lake . . .

>   mountain . . . water . . .

There will always be change

And if these do not last

Do man's visions last?

Do man's illusions?

During the session

Take things as they come

All things pass

—Psychedelic Prayers

22

CAPTURE

I was a man without a country. An Orange County district attorney boasted to having indicted me on 19 counts of drug trafficking. The Swiss would not extend further asylum to me. My future looked bleak.

Joanna Harcourt-Smith and I fled to Afghanistan early in 1973, where I was kidnapped at gun point by American agents at the Kabul airport and turned over to U.S. drug enforcement agents. I was taken back to Orange County to be tried for escape. I was easily convicted and sentenced to five years, in addition to my two previous ten-year sentences. I also faced 11 counts from the second Millbrook bust and 19 conspiracy counts related to my indictment as the head of a drug-smuggling outfit. I was facing some 95 years in prison.

Intelligence Agents

In Afghanistan with Joanna

The fugitive philosopher had become the most dangerous man in the USA. The sentencing judge remarked, "If he is allowed to travel freely, he will speak publicly and spread his ideas." The effectiveness of the philosopher could be measured in the severity of his punishment for voicing his ideas. To make sure that I could further spread my influence, I was put into solitary confinement in Folsom Prison.

Monastic Life

My monastic life started in the Spring of 1973. As long as Ronald Reagan was governor of California and Richard Nixon was in charge of federal matters, it seemed obvious that I would remain in prison. The way to get through bad times is to spin a cocoon, which we learned from the social insects—the oldest and wisest of civilized species.

It turned out that Folsom Prison was an ideal place to hibernate. The California Department of Corrections kept me in solitary confinement for 29 months, which was the ultimate neurological luxury. Years later when journalists asked, "How were you affected by so many months of solitary confinement?" I always answered light-heartedly, "My cellmate was one of the funniest, creative minds in the prison."

It turned out that Folsom Prison was an ideal place to hibernate.

Sitting on the cement floor of a roach-ridden cell, I wrote *Neurologic* on the back of a humorless legal brief and smuggled it out to a lawyer who assured me that his Hindu guru was meditating actively in my defense.

This little pamphlet was reprinted in its entirety in two national magazines and republished in dozens of small-press formats. Well over 100,000 copies were thus blown around the world.

TIMOTHY LEARY/JAIL NOTES
INTRODUCTION   ALLEN GINSBERG

All my books have covered the same territory: the epic voyage of evolution, step-by-step improvement in our neurotechnology, which is taking us from precambrian bliss to fusion in some ultimate violet whole. Why not? *Neurologic* summarized many years of rumination about the stages of evolving neurotechnology, here centered on the 8 ecologies: 4 terrestrial—marine, land, tribal-artifact, urban; and 4 post—terrestrial: body, brain, DNA, and atomic nuclear. In later books, *Exo-Psychology, Neuropolitics, Intelligence Agents,* and *Game of Life,* these 8 circuits were expanded to 24 more-detailed stages of human evolution.

Reading it now, I am aware of the hopeful, almost prescientific naivete. The seminal works of Gerard O'Neill on space colonization, the great neurochemistry breakthroughs that taught us that the brain is a wondrous gland, always producing its own entertaining secretions, the vistas of sociobiology, the wizard microgenetics of the human leucocyte antigen community, the histo-compatability, and recombinant DNA heroes—all were outside my sphere of cheerful ignorance. But the basic navigational coordinates were fairly well outlined.

–Changing My Mind Among Others

Out Castes may endure **long** periods of quescence, obscurity, and even disgrace.

–Intelligence Agents

23
LETTER FROM BRIAN BARRITT

*i*n September 1973 a letter from Brain Barritt arrived when I was in Folsom Prison: Nice to know you're OK and reassuring to know that your nervous system is in your control and mind functioning with the same sizzle as always. Christ man, the three months I just finished in the Amsterdam jail were longer than the three years I did in England. Prison is a bore but it does get the extrasensory mechanisms moving. Helps to catch up with the reading too; I read all the English books in the library, murder, rape, robbery, all the things a good con should know. Even found a copy of Bucke's *Cosmic Consciousness*—for long termers, I guess.

The last few weeks I was the only English speaking guy in the place. The Silent One wandering through the prison structure like a spectre with the three dumb monkeys on my back "Saying Nothing, Understanding Nothing, Contributing Nothing" except a few words in pidgin Dutch and an occasional bleep of enthusiasm. Then they let me out, steal my money and buy me a ticket on the first boat to England. In the detention cell at the Hook of Holland I meet her, Jane, seventeen years young and it's her first deportation, she's traveling back on the night boat, the same boat as meeeee!

Well, like it's just cosmically planned baby, that's all. I am showing her the constellations as we cruise beneath the occult moon before she tells me she is a boy! Total embarrassment, absolute disorientation! Just what a con needs on his first night out.

So many odd and funny things happened to me from when I was deported till I arrived back in Holland with a fresh passport 48 hours later. Even the fuzz goofed and paid me 50 pounds by mistake. Omens coming in thick and fast, Bonne Chance to rebirth.

Business Section

You asked about Michel Hauchard. I made no agreements, settlements, with him. We got photostats of the correspondence between the lawyers and our suit against him was coming together nicely when Hauchard split the country. I didn't have the bread to chase him around France. With a little help from Joanna I might have been able to do more but my letters asking for information were unanswered or the content ignored. When you were in Afghan I told Michel he could keep the quarter of a million from Bantam and no hassles from our side concerning the rights to your future works, if he got you out of custody or delayed your flight back to the States. Later when Sue was in Amsterdam I offered to drop the case against him if he sent her $5,000. Nothing was put in writing. He did not help in any way.

Sounds:

David Bowie

Literature

Simone Vinkenoog **translated** *Confessions of a Hope Fiend* into Dutch. I am going to Switzerland—soon as Davie Log has finished his holidays and is back

in England for the new term. To see what is happening
to *The Psychedelic Prayers*. Carl Lazlo says the publisher
still owes money to the printer and is having trouble
with distribution—as always. A photostat version of
Neurologic has been done in German by Gruner Zweig.
I'm glad to see the Germans are on to it.

Personal

Met Elizabeth's father. Sergeant Pepper himself. All
the guys of his generation have minds like the *Ency-
clopaedia Britannica*. So I'm sipping my sherry and trying not to look too sexy when it strikes me that this
sprightly old rooster is ogling his daughter. He was
so jealous, man I was amazed. I am sexually ignorant
about father/daughter relationships but I can tell
when a guy is aching to fuck my chick and Dr. El-
liott-Cooke is coming on with a heavy bedside man-
ner. Liz thinks it's all a gas but I don't think he'll ever
make her. Not with those classical sounds anyhow.

When I reflect on it, incest seems a good idea. I
believe it to be an evolutionary method for strengthening existing genetic combinations. All the animals
do it now and again to purify and reinforce herd
characteristics. Inbreeding is a stabilizing force, a
survival factor designed to balance out the evolutionary pressures that cause
constant change in the species,
but for God's sake don't tell
anyone. How the incest taboo
came about I've no idea, but it
came early on when the earth
needed populating and as
much variation as possible was needed so that evolution could get moving, and I see no reason for this
archaic Pre-Cambrian attitude to continue.

> Inbreeding is a sta-
> bilizing force, a sur-
> vival factor designed
> to balance out the
> evolutionary pressures.

Brian Barritt

Intelligence Agents

The City

Feeling very immortal lately with my lotus feet in high-heeled silver boots, ice cream coat, white satin drape, and thoughts going off like fireworks. But without each other to orient by, Elizabeth and myself would have difficulty in keeping our Circuit 6 Show free from the terrestrial realities whirlpooling around us.

Adam is a whirlpool of cults, scenes and shows. Magicians have been laying down these trips since '66 and disoriented time travelers come spiraling into the city and zapp into some mind-web or other before they can get a psychological bearing.

Adam is like living an immense brain. Really, Tim, it's very moving to see how the Time Underground has nurtured this incredible being. The visions we saw in the early 60s are a living entity now. Sci-Fiction monsters that turned out to be friendly after all. Oh, it's wearing patched jeans and it's broke most of the time, but in terms of human relationships it's the deepest and most profound model ever.

At present Adam has the highest mass consciousness on the planet. I doubt whether it will survive the leap from Circuit 5 to Circuit 6 and still head the evolutionary thrust, but at this moment, before the first neurological city is pinpointed, Adam acts as the model point of the earth's spiritual energy supply. A most intelligent comment. Barritt knows that a neurogenetic migration is in the air. Like a good Evolutionary Agent he inquires about the next ecological niche.

Feeling immortal with my lotus feet in high-heeled silver boots, ice cream coat, white satin drape, and thoughts going off like fireworks.

Well, as you see, we are in love with the city and the city is in love with us. We have not too much difficulty relating to the authorities in this setting, but one foot over the Dutch border in any direction and the pressure is full on against us. Your letter says, "It is very good not to be in an adversary position with the law." But Tim, it's the law that's in

The Dutch have respect for the intelligence of some non-conformists; they have seen many pleasant changes and Holland has a history as a refuge for the persecuted.

an adversary position to us. I can't remember ever having committed a crime by my DNA standards. I therefore figure I ain't committed any crimes. The closer I follow my nervous system—the Buzz—the more I am in tune with the evolutionary goal, it would be a crime if I did otherwise. A common complaint of futique mutants who cannot gear inner to outer; who fail to realize that each stage must be externally mastered and used as launching pad; that each hive establishment must be re-assured.

The "straight" world is amiable here. The Underground and hippies are often treated with respect. The Netherlanders are an easy-going race at heart and since millions of guilders pour into the country via young cats who come to smoke the almost legal pot, the burly burghers of protestant Holland have a civic duty to respect their strange modes of dress and ultra-violet hair—as long as they have bread.

But it is more than that, really. It's not just bread that motivates the Dutch amiability. They have respect for the intelligence of some non-conformists; they have seen many pleasant changes and Holland has a history as a refuge for the persecuted. The Pilgrim Fathers stayed here a while after being pressurized

out of England. It has a lot in common with Switzerland as a harbor of safety as well. And on the other
side of the coin Sergius Golowin tells me the Dutch
hired the Swiss mercenaries to capture the East In-
dies for them.

Sometimes glimpses of the year 2000 appear through
chinks in the city's time stream, electromagnetic
love-songs drilling through the streets, reflecting in
the canals, twining fleur-de-lys round the spires of
Baroque churches, the feeling of family, the strong
warm glow of "home." Electric symbiosis. Comfort-
ing force fields of mutual respect.

Notes

Mutation does not happen by accident, it happens to those who put themselves in the position and place
where maximum possibilities for change can occur, after
that it's just a matter of Bonne Chance.

How to Get Your Ego Back

Love thyself, and then find someone you like better.

Something's in the air. Since we received your letter we
have had visitors from Swiss every week inquiring about
you. Giger, Sergius, Carl Laslo, Brummbaer and this week
Kristoff from the Hesse-Haus in Corona.
I think your time in prison is nearing an
end.

Love thyself, and then find someone you like better.

Simone Vinkenoog suggests that I start
a correspondence with you with the view
of publishing later. If you think it's a good
idea we'll do it, just let me know which questions to ask
you.

Brummbaer is a first class artist. As soon as I get some slides I will send you them. I am very impressed by his work; there's softness, tenderness, strength and humor in them. They are healthy pictures. We neurologicians badly need a coherent symbol system. The "occultist" has a wealth of traditional symbols to call on. The eastern trip is alive with radiant images. The neurologician has nothing really beautiful to look at. There are too few Sci-Fi artists about. What is needed is contemporary illustrations, parables to the alchemical and eastern ones. I put some of Brummbaer's pictures in the pages of *Terra II* and the book blossomed from an Underground production into a jewel-like scripture.

Imagery is very important right now. How about a mandala like the Buddhist Wheel of Becoming with the eight circuits illustrated so that the whole system can be taken in at once? Hedonic textbook? Cats are tripping out on Hindu and Buddhist symbols when they should be building up memory archives based on contemporary and futique views of the scene.

Have you designed Tarot cards yet? If you have something in mind, flash me and I will ask Brummbaer to do it. Posters are a quick way of telling people that a contemporary religion/philosophy exists. Everybody has been waiting for a neurological Tarot for ages and a science-fiction will become standard equipment for time travelers.

Our experimental tolerances have reached immense proportions. We are having difficulty finding enough stimuli to satisfy our habits. Really, we need freezing till 2000 and waking up when the earth's intensity ratio has risen a few points. This is the highest point of Old Brain thinking. The New Brain response is: Brian, don't be so passive. Swim West and carpenter the future. However, as *Terra II* gets nearer to the White Hole at the center of our galaxy and the stars

Swim West and carpenter the future.

I make my entrance wearing my ice cream coat of vivid satin and silver high-heeled boots, Liz in amber and gold, red high-heels, smoking a phosphorescent cigarette.

are more numerous, we should meet and exchange information with other extra-terrestrials and the most sophisticated ecstasies of the Milky Way will be at our disposal. Unparalleled joys will streak and sizzle along our ganglia while Nirvana's and Satori's crackle and pop and awesome blue-white blasts murmur extra sensory obscenities to our souls. Progress is measured here in terms of how much ecstasy can you take on the Pleasure Meters of Total Bliss.

I make my entrance wearing my ice cream coat of vivid satin and silver high-heeled boots, Liz in amber and gold, red high-heels, smoking a phosphorescent cigarette.

We enter from opposite sides of the stage, meet in the middle, kiss, and merge into electrical life from flashing zigzags of lightning. The lightning forks; we exchange bodies. I am Liz. She is me. The lightning slows to a pulsing golden glow as we divide into our two separate forms. We are looking at each other out of each others' eyes, we are the same entity and also two different entities at the same time. I take a draw on my cigarette. Brian blows a kiss to the audience, we exit together in a shower of stardust.

Bye Time
Love, Bonne Chance

Brian

−Intelligence Agents

The fugitive professor eXpounds upon The Secrets.

Diane Dorr Dorynek (from *Intelligence Agents*)

Live your highest vision.
–Your Brain Is God

Think for Yourself

QUESTION AUTHORITY

*T*hroughout human history, as our species has faced the frightening, terrorizing
fact that we do not know who we are, or where
we're going in this ocean of chaos. The political,
the religious, the educational authorities have attempted to comfort us by giving us order, rules,
regulations—in-forming—forming in our minds
their view of reality.

To think for yourself you must question authority.

To think for yourself you must learn to put
yourself in a state of vulnerable open-mindedness
—chaotic, confused vulnerability—
to inform yourself.

—*Intelligence Agents*

Different
Venerations
For
Different
Generations

–Intelligence Agents

Grow with the Flow!

–Your Brain Is God

24

PARABLE OF THE INFORMER

It was not a secret that the Weather Underground had enabled me to escape. They proudly took the credit they deserved and wanted. I sent a query to the Weather Underground through a sympathetic prisoner that I was being pressured into making a deal with the FBI and waited for their approval. The return message was "we understand." Many of my good friends didn't, however.

In July 1974 I was taken in handcuffs to Terminal Island, a Federal prison, and placed in the "hole." The hole was the name of the punishment cell-block. When I protested I was told that I was being kept off the main-line because my sentence, which was ten years for the possession of a half-ounce of marijuana, was too lengthy for a medium-security prison.

An informer is one who communicates facts that someone else, usually a bureaucrat, does not want communicated.

I was then visited by a notorious hard ass Federal agent, who made the following statement: "If you double-cross me I'll have you put on the main-line of a Federal Prison with the jacket of a snitch. Do you know what that means?" I nodded that I understood the threat.

Actually, I was in prison for acting as an "informer." An informer is one who communicates facts that someone else, usually a bureaucrat, does not want communicated. I had publicized information about human intelligence, which certain espionage agencies and information bureaus wanted to keep secret. That's how I got to be the most dangerous man alive.

Gravity's Rainbow

On the second day of my incarceration in the "hole" I asked for reading material. An hour later I heard the padlock and the rasp of the metal slot being opened. I passively accepted a book which was pushed through the slot. It was entitled *Gravity's Rainbow*. The author was Thomas Pynchon. One quick glance sufficed for me to understand that the book was an important signal.

I lay on the bed and read for 12 hours until the lights were turned off. The next morning I woke at sunrise and read for 15 hours. The following morning I finished the first reading, promptly turned back to page one and spent two days re-reading and annotating. During the subsequent week, I decoded, outlined and charted the narrative. Every character in *Gravity's Rainbow* is either an operative working for a psycho-political hive-bureaucracy or an independent intelligent agent—an out-caste—working to counter hive-bureaucracy.

Charles Thrush

My tactics placed me in "Their" hands to find out who They were and how They operated. Thus my task in the Federal Prison system was surveillance.

WOULD YOU VOLUNTARILY STAY IN PRISON - FOR LIFE - FOR YOUR IDEAS?

SURVEILLANCE: Close observation of a person or group especially of one under suspicion.

SURVEILLANT: One who keeps a close watch; French present particle (sic) of surveiller, to watch over. Sur, on top of or over + veiller, from vigil, awake, watchful.

I was taken from a cell in Terminal Island Prison at 3:00 A.M. by two armed Federal Agents and driven to the Los Angeles airport. I was told only that I was traveling under an alias and that if I attempted to escape, I would be shot. I was flown to Minneapolis and picked up by two Federal agents who drove me to the Federal Prison in Sandstone, Minnesota. Upon arrival I was taken to the warden's office and told that I was to be admitted to the prison under an alias. I protested to the warden that this was a perilous act and demanded that I be registered under my own name. The warden replied that he had no choice but to follow orders. No choice but to follow orders!

I was told that my name was Charles Thrush. The thrush is a song bird.

I was told that my name was Charles Thrush. The thrush is a song bird.

It was Friday evening, no appeal of this decision could be made to Washington. I was conducted to the "hole" and locked in a small metal room with no furnishings except a mattress and bedding. The metal door to the cell had a slot 8 inches high and 24 inches in width. The slot was secured from the outside by a padlock. At meal times and at various times during the day and night, a guard unlocked the slot—that according to Solzhenitsyn, Soviet prisoners call "The Swine Trough". At one such inspection, I asked the guard what my name was. I was told that my name was Charles Thrush. The thrush is a song bird.

–Intelligence Agents

Decline

of LSD Boom

*C*onservatives are quick to point out that transcendental, self-indulgent movements usually lead to the fall of civilizations. Did not hot tubs, Eastern drugs, and mystical cults sap the martial vigor of Imperial Rome?

Probably. But we must hasten to add that it was natural and right that Rome fall. In the unbroken migration of intelligence and individual freedom from east to west, Rome had its day in the sun. Would you want to be ruled today from Italy? High civilizations do not fall; they blossom and send their seed pollens westward. Have not the descendants of the witty Sicilian Italians planted their roots today in Hollywood and Las Vegas? According to such observers as Kissinger, Herman Kahn, Reverend Falwell, and the Shah of Iran, our current hedonic drug culture represents a sophisticated corruption of the puritan American ethos. But in their self-serving zeal to restore the old morality, these imperialists fail to realize that hedonic movements go through predictable states of growth just like other social phenomena, and that the American transcendentalism has hardly gotten started.

> Hippies were the first naive, innocent, idealistic babies of the new neurological information society.

Hippies were the first naive, innocent, idealistic babies of the new neurological information society. They were passive consumers of the new technology, childish utopians believing tie-dyed clothes, Grateful Dead concerts, and parroted love slogans were the ultimate flowers of evolution.

The hippie wave declined because its members were too passive, opting for enlightenment at the nearest dealer's pad. Advertising usually does get ahead of production in the development of new culture-changing technologies, and I am ready to accept responsibility for that. No blame, though. When a species wants an evolutionary tool, it will get it in a generation or two. By 1970 there were, apparently, some seven million lazy consumers expecting to be given the easy ticket to brain change. Meanwhile the feds had snuffed out the few reliable manufacturers. Predictably, the land was flooded with unreliable, low-quality acid. Good-hearted amateurs combined with unscrupulous scoundrels to distribute an inferior product

Thus the wholesome decline in LSD use, which stimulated exactly what the drug culture needed. Smarten up, Sister. Smarten-up, Brother! People were no longer so naively utopian. They warily thought twice before tripping. And the challenge, which no sophisticated chemist could resist, to produce high-quality LSD, was thrown down.

–Chaos & Cyber Culture

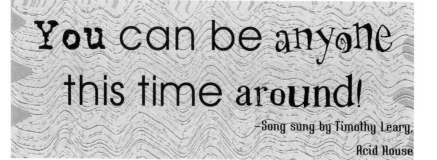

You can be anyone this time around!

–Song sung by Timothy Leary,

Acid House

S.M.i^2.L.E.

SM—Space Migration
i^2—Intelligence Increase
LE—Life Extension

—Intelligence Agents

QUESTION AUTHORITY

It's Legal
To S.M.I²:L.E. Again

After my release from prison in April, 1976, I traveled extensively around the U. S. checking on the intelligence quotient of America. I have a few hot items to report back to you. Number one, there's a Good Feeling running rampant in this country. There is a feeling of gentleness, an expectation of change, a hedonic hope reminiscent in many ways of those tender years in the early sixties. You know, just a few years ago if you smiled a lot you were in danger of being busted on suspicion. Today it is legal, my fellow Americans, to smile once again. Here's why: flower children have turned on, booted up and are taking over.

Flower children have turned on, booted up and taken over.

The prohibition against New Ideas has been repealed so we can get together to see what further agitation we can stir up. Corporations, governments agencies, and heads of state (no pun intended) through out America and Europe have been taken over by successful Heads of the sixties. Articulate young women and men who were forced by our government into positions of dissent and protest have dropped back in. For a number of years now they have been managing, directing and taking responsibility for affairs. This bloodless coup, this quiet revolution is no surprise. It was predictable. The neuropolitical experiment we started at Harvard in 1960 was a success! I remember a 1968 Gallup finding that 75% of Harvard law students were smoking grass. So it was predictable that my legal problems would be over ten years later—1978.

The same Gallup poll reported that 75% of pre-medical students were smoking grass. Soon we had a new generation of young doctors sensitized to the beauty of childbirth; physicians who understand that pregnancy is not a disease to be terminated by an obstetrical operation. Similar changes transformed other professions. Even the dismal but exciting trade of law enforcement has been taken over by young women and men who lived through the explosive sixties and cultivated a new sense of human relativity. Now we have a new breed of turned-on cops. The 1968 Gallup poll also reported that 65% of the science and engineering students at MIT, Cal-Tech, and RPI were smoking grass. Thus, for the first time, we have a new generation of young scientists who have experienced in their own nervous systems the genetic, biological and physical energies they study in the laboratories.   *–Intelligence Agents*

The prohibition against New Ideas has been repealed so let's get together to see what further agitation we can stir up.

East is behind us—the past.
West is before us—the future.

America is the genetic frontier.

Go West young Wo-Man!

–Intelligence Agents

All **suffering** is caused by being in the **wrong place.**

Solution➪Move!

—Intelligence Agents

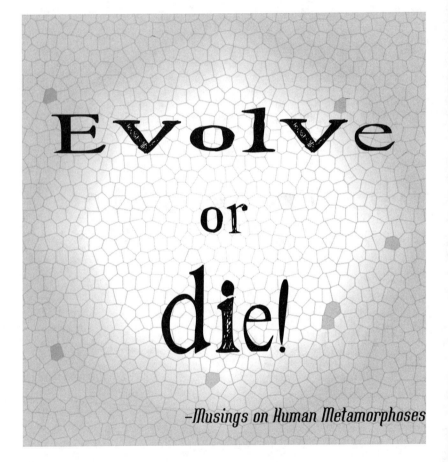

Evolve or die!

—Musings on Human Metamorphoses

25

IN THE END

i **got involved** in a little struggle in the 1960s. East
versus West. A simple Genetic Super-bowl competition for the consciousness of a small planet. Past
versus Future. Washington Senators versus the California
Angels. I got put in the penalty box for four years and
spent three more years in twenty nine jails in California's
prison system until Governor Jerry Brown released me on
April 21, 1976.

Drugs and drug abuse influenced me throughout
life—privately and publicly, personally and professionally.
The most damaging incidents in my life were intertwined
with booze. Liquor spoiled my father's life and the lives of
four uncles. Alcohol was behind Marianne's suicide and
the unraveling of friendships. I ingested enormous quanti-
ties of psychedelic drugs—particularly LSD and cannabis.
Unlike with booze, I have no regrets about anything I ever
did while "tripping". My experiences with these chemicals were quiet, serene, humorous, sensual, and reflective.
They made me a better person whereas too much booze
sometimes lead to eruptions of vulgarity, insensitivity and
aggression.

High Priest

Throughout my professional life I followed the athletic model: players, coaches, teams, leagues. I organized my work as psychologist and philosopher by the same principles. I tried many life games, seeking out those I wanted to become proficient at. Infield, outfield—I selected certain positions to master. Then I got the best coaching available and practiced, practiced, practiced. Improved. Excelled. And I kept changing the game. Winning is a short-range concept, suspect and often irrelevant. I always aimed to move on to more complex games.

−Timothy Leary

Turn On
Tune In
Drop Out

More Ronin Books
by Timothy Leary

Recommended

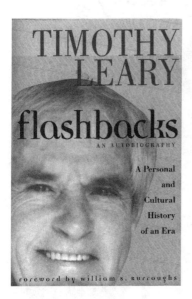

Flashbacks
An Autobiography

by Timothy Leary
Foreword: Burroughs
Tarcher/Putnam

isbn 0-87477-870-0

I Have America Surrounded
The Life of Timothy Leary

by John Higgs
Foreword: Winona Ryder
Barricade Legend
isbn 978-1-56980-315-8

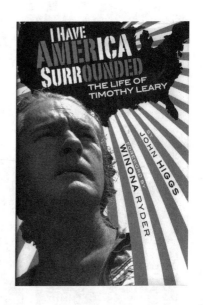

Ronin Books for Independent

Question Authority

Think for Yourself